Are Sa

NOT ON THIS BOARD YOU DON'T

Making Your Trustees More Effective

Arthur C. Frantzreb

Bonus Books, Inc., Chicago

01   00   99   98   97   5   4   3   2   1

Library of Congress Cataloging-in-Publication Data

Frantzreb, Arthur C.
    Not on this board you don't : making your trustees more effective /
Arthur C. Frantzreb.
        p.   cm.
    Includes bibliographical references and index.
    ISBN 1-56625-067-6
    1. Directors of corporations.   2. Trusts and trustees.   I. Title.
HD2745.F7   1996
658.4'22—dc21   96-46282

Bonus Books, Inc.
160 East Illinois Street
Chicago, Illinois 60611

Printed in the United States of America

Table of Contents

❦

Acknowledgments

It is impossible for me to even begin to estimate how many persons over the years have urged me to publish a book or two or three — staff members, client trustees, executives, proteges who have excelled, friends, and family. I owe so much to all of these wonderful friends.

But one friend especially stands out — J. Mark Lono. It was he who over a year ago called me and said: "Art, it's time that you had a book available to our world of philanthropic organizations. How would it be if I suggested an outline for you?" That did it! It took me only a moment to say "Yes." We spent a couple of days together reviewing all of my materials from over the years and then three weeks later the table of contents arrived.

Mark Lono is a professional's professional. We worked closely together when he was vice president of the University of Tampa. He has had quite a career before and since.

Then there's Jerold Panas, a famous consultant, writer, and friend of long standing who turned his publisher loose on me.

What you see and what you read started in 1948. Upon my graduation from Butler University in Indianapolis, I was persuaded by Carl W. Shaver to join his firm, Marts and Lundy, Inc., then of New York City. He asked me to serve with him in his direction of Cornell University's four phase, $90,250,000, 10-year Greater Cornell Fund program, one of the early important university capital campaigns after World

War II. I accepted the offer and graduated from Butler in absentia so that I could be on Cornell's campus on June 1, 1948.

Carl had served as director of the public relations department under me when I was Camp Sergeant Major of the Transportation Corps Replacement Training Center at Camp Plauche in New Orleans. Both he and I went on to receive our commissions.

The unique experience at Cornell, working at a top staff level and later as regional director in Northern New Jersey, was an incredible life-changing experience. Carl was my supervisor and my inspiration. Those early, wonderful days, now nearly 50 years ago, caused me to dedicate my life to the ministry of philanthropic productivity for humanitarian purposes.

It is now more than 850 clients, hundreds of speeches and articles later. This book summarizes and projects experiences for others to follow in the fulfillment of creative philanthropic achievements in our ever-changing society. I shall forever be in the debt of all these remarkable men and women, and I take this opportunity now to acknowledge their gift to me.

Introduction

My business life has been dedicated to helping people help people in nonprofit organizations which exist for humanitarian purposes. Whether governing board members, staff executive officers, staff implementators, volunteers, or gift or grant prospects, each person has talents, skills, integrity, creativity, and a spiritual capacity to help others. While these characteristics exist, the question is always *how to mobilize these assets to sponsor greater and greater philanthropic productivity.*

When I came into this management field, there were no general workshops or seminars like we have today in the Indiana University Center on Philanthropy in Indianapolis. There, as part of the Center, is the national fund raising school founded by Henry A. Rosso. Before, the kind of training, education, and advice that the school provided was achieved only by experience and guidance from mentor models. Then came experience, observation, analyses, and progress. And with these achievements came counsel and counsellors.

The chief role of truly experienced counsellors is to advise institutions and organizations what "not to do" to achieve their vision, mission, goals, and objectives. To be a counsellor is like being a healthcare specialist. When one goes to such a specialist, it is hoped that one does not receive the prescription just given to the previous patient.

When one becomes a nonprofit counsellor to advise on how to achieve philanthropic productivity goals, that person must be a sensitive, honest, creative, observant analyst of what it takes to become the best counsellor one can be. Herein lies my motive: to be creative, not repetitive; to be helpful to those who can help others to make a difference; to persuade the proper persons to serve as investment counsellors for gift and grant results, not just fund raisers; to serve really as ministers of the results of philanthropic investments.

Contained in this book is a comprehensive collation and digestion of positions, procedures, practices, and policies which I have successfully applied to diverse nonprofit organizations.

Herein is a personal biography of applied counsel. Every organization, every person, every situation, every result is different. This reminds me of the historic definition of fund raising: "A series of disappointments sprinkled with a few brilliant successes, most of which were not expected."

Counsellors make the difference in advising what to do if confidence in investments is expected for fiscal stability and security.

To Begin

Philanthropy in the United States is big business, a major industry touching every American. The impact of this industry is approaching $150 billion a year and it will go higher. A study shows that at least $100 billion more is available today from living personal and family resources. Historically, individuals and families have accounted for 85 to 90 percent of all resources given annually. Hence, the basis for considering philanthropy as a ministry in meeting diverse humanitarian needs. The word "philanthropy" comes from the Greek *philos anthropos,* meaning "love for man," "love for mankind," "love for humankind."

This rather quiet but persistent industry is presided over by tens of thousands of America's best and brightest solid citizens dedicated only to the visions and missions of the individual organizations, the betterment of society locally and generally, and to the best interests of beneficiaries of their applied programs and services.

Why, then, are so many of the intentions inefficient, duplicative? The managers of every charitable organization are the governing boards. Such boards are created as a public trust by the not-for-profit corporate statutes of every state. Hence, such statutes should identify such boards as boards of trustees, not boards of directors.

Yet, trustees of religious, educational, healthcare, human service, cultural, societal benefit, environmental, international and other nonprofit groups far too often do not know exactly and honestly what their job is; what their obligations, responsibilities, and accountability factors are; and how they are supposed to function individually and jointly. Above all, a board of trustees was never designed to be just another for-profit board of directors!

Today, trustees watch dumbfounded as the New Era scam and the United Way trustee embarrassments unfold and other unethical and conflict-of-interest revelations are revealed. They haven't a clue about the state statutes governing their existence. They haven't a clue about what their staff is really up to. They haven't a clue about how their organization functions internally or externally. They haven't a clue about what their organization is really all about. With that information, each member can be counted upon to serve as a knowledgeable public advocate.

Good folks who scrutinize their businesses, worry about their own families, second-guess their favorite sports team, and hold their politicians accountable often figuratively take a walk from the heady responsibilities of trusteeship, which they volunteered to undertake.

In the Beginning

Individuals who see a person's, family's or civic need and desire to assist in relieving that need can form a group of citizens to meet that need. This is philanthropy in action — people caring for people. This is positive, applied philanthropy in sharing time, talents, and personal treasure for others.

This is what happened when the early Pilgrims landed on our shores. When a problem existed, neighbors cared for their neighbors. No community, no county, or state organization existed to aid citizens in need of food, housing, clothing or illnesses. There were no governments. There was no American Red Cross or Salvation Army. There were no charitable organizations except religious. People cared for people who might in turn be called to help them someday.

Then these groups became formalized. As those groups grew, the founders segregated themselves into a controlling committee with rules and regulations. Their volunteer services became organized to meet a public good. Communities became formalized. Towns were formed. Cities were formed. States were formed. Lawyers found their mission.

Thus our two-million-plus nonprofit charity groups were formed under boards whose members joined hand-in-hand, heart-to-heart to help others in need. At the same time, millions of business firms formed groups to sell products and services benefiting their group and other stockholders as stakeholders when customers and clients called upon them.

Then government stepped in. And with government, attorneys. And with attorneys, regulations for public control.

These groups became formalized as boards, and boards were cited as being obligated, responsible, and accountable for meeting ethical management guidelines for mission achievements, policies, procedures, personnel, production of services, and fiscal stability and security.

As needs grew, organizations grew in number. Boards grew as did the need for more volunteers and financial support to meet greater humanitarian needs for greater populations. Then came the necessity for certification of group values, missions, programs, and ethical procedures. Every state required applications for approval of articles of incorporation to validate the existence of the group as a noncommercial, volunteer-centered, public service provider. Then the federal government encouraged individuals, families, businesses, and others to give their fiscal resources to the state-approved organization as tax-exempt gifts to prevent the government from having to step in to tax everyone for meeting public needs. Thus, nonprofit, volunteer-centered, public service entities became tax exempt under stringent regulations, and donor investors found that voluntary gifts were tax deductible from their annual and estate resources.

Know What a Board is Not

What do you mean we're a public trust?

Perhaps the greatest shock that I have witnessed among governing board members as well as chief executive officers is the revelation that not-for-profit corporations are public trusts. When such organizations are created for public philanthropic purposes rather than stockholder purposes, they function to serve the public of the incorporating state and are accountable to the public of the state first. Unfortunately, too few states enforce that accountability.

The governing board of nonprofit organizations exist as state-approved public trusts. Such trusts are not the same as for-profit boards of directors. Trustee boards are not the "owners" of their organization as are stock-holding directors of for-profit businesses. Trustees must provide personal gifts for the budgets they approve and pay for attending meetings. Directors get paid for being directors, for attending meetings, and through diverse fringe benefits.

The minimum board membership required for a nonprofit organization are the three persons required by the articles of incorporation in every state but two. The other two states require only one person as founding incorporator. Therefore, given a vision for creating a nonprofit organization; given resolution of a mission to be fulfilled; given purpose, goals, and objectives to be accomplished, why does any organization need more governing board members than those required by state statutory law? Numbers of members has never been the answer for viability and insurability for founding and funding to meet human needs. Here the oft-quoted Rule of Thirds stands as immortal:

> In any group of people, one-third will respond to the purpose for which they were called far, far beyond expectations of performance; one-third will respond only to the liberal application of a rusty needle; and the last third will never respond as promised.

When governing board members of nonprofit organizations are made aware of the import of their obligations and responsibilities as trustees of a public trust, their whole attitude changes about their acceptance of the invitation to become a trustee and of their personal responsibility. (Even their facial expressions change.) Their first question after this revelation is, "Why didn't someone tell me about the importance of this position?" Then, "Why isn't it in our bylaws?" And so on.

Two basic points are in these questions. First, the presumption of having responsibility for the management of a public trust appears as an awesome assignment without experience. Second is the appearance that being a member of a nonprofit governing board isn't as serious or impelling as that of a public trust.

The real basic problems of nonprofit governing board membership are:

1. seldom does any nonprofit organization have in the office of the chief executive an up-to-date copy of the pertinent state statutes regarding not-for-profit corporations to share with board members;
2. never are potential board members shown or made aware of these statutes;
3. never are potential board members shown or made aware of the original and/or changes to the basic articles of incorporation whose power precedes any subsequent bylaw;
4. never are the governing state statutes or articles of incorporation referred to in the board bylaws as factors preceding any bylaw management provisions;
5. never are the pertinent state statutes or articles of incorporation appended to up-to-date bylaws now included in governing board operating manuals;
6. seldom is there a description of each position on the governing board based upon nonprofit state statutes;
7. seldom are governing board members provided with up-to-date bylaws;
8. seldom do bylaws show dates of total governing board approval or signature of the board secretary, officer or board chair.

9. seldom do bylaws contain statute provisions for conflicts of interest or indemnification of members; and
10. almost never are board members given copies of the Internal Revenue Service letter citing officially the organization's tax-exempt status.

Yet, these board members, each with the best possible intentions and commitment, serve and serve well in a social sense but are totally unaware of their legal expectancy as managers of a public trust.

Both fortunately and unfortunately, most states are lax in evaluating both for-profit and not-for-profit legal operations.

But how would your board members change their attitudes; implement their professed commitment; and devote real time, talent, and personal treasure if they knew and accepted their role as members of a public trust, plus assisting and providing human services? Yes, if some members knew their legal expectancy, they would resign and that could be their greatest contribution.

Trustees or Directors: Which is Which?

The majority of the governing boards of the independent sector, not-for-profit, tax-exempt, charitable organizations are referred to as boards of trustees or boards of directors. Some are called boards of regents, boards of governors, and related terms. However, most are boards of trustees or directors. In concept, in practice, in perceptions, and at law there is a difference between the term "trustee" and the term "director." Then why are so many charitable organizations headed by a board of directors? The statutes of these charitable organizations are prepared by attorneys and law clerks inexperienced in the art — if not the science — of managing two different kinds of corporate bodies. These same persons prepare bylaws, not as managers of different corporate bodies, but the same provisions for all: profit-making or nonprofit, each of which is different in personal criteria, perceptions, and social impact. Let's look at the definitions of trustee and director representing a composite of resources.

Trustee/Trustees. A person or body requested to serve terms as concerned and committed voluntary managers of a statutory public trust for the public good; and a trust of the human, physical, and fiscal resources given or committed to the body for health, religious, cultural, educational, humanitarian, social or other beneficiaries as philanthropies serving the public in lieu of or in addition to governments.

Director/Directors. A person or body consisting of appointed staff officers and others of prominence and/or distinction who hold, acquire, and/or are given shares of stock and are provided with salaries and/or payments for services rendered plus fringe and auxiliary benefits having a direct and general management and fiduciary relationship to the corporation to insure production and profitability.

Governing board members — nonprofit or for-profit (except for business owners) — are selected because of the direct or implied benefit their position, experience, talent, judgment, wisdom, influence, affluence or skills helps to ensure benefits to the organization.

Let's look at trustees and directors in a different form:

For-Profit Business Directors *Differences*	*Similarities*	**Nonprofit Organization Trustees** *Differences*
1. Executive officers become members	1. Created by state statutes	1. Executive officers never members except as *ex officio*
2. Members own or can own stock	2. Governed first by state statutes	2. Members are volunteers from constituencies

3. Members are paid fees or salaries	3. Responsible, obligated, and accountable to provisions of state statutes	3. Members must personally give to budgets they approve
4. Concerned primarily with production and profit to stockholders	4. Accountable to federal laws, regulations, and tax provisions	4. Concerned for excellence in human services and balanced budgets
5. Appointees connote commercial impact to stockholders	5. Become public/ constituent representatives	5. Electees connote confidence for advocacy, access, and mission fulfillment
6. Benefits from ample staff experience and implementation	6. Connotes personal fulfillment of achievement	6. Operate with limited staff for policy implementation
7. Subject to and wary of competition	7. Sets, oversees, and evaluates policy implementation	7. Function as philanthropies
8. Initiates costly research and studies	8. Affected by involuntary social issues, forces, and trends	8. Must obtain grants for innovation, research, and studies
9. Obtains new fiscal resources by marketing stock	9. Subject to public acceptance for services or products	9. Looks to endowment for fiscal stability and security

Given the features and factors contained herein, let's call the governing boards of our two-million-plus nonprofit charitable organizations and institutions **boards of trustees.**

Let's communicate to the members their public trust responsibilities.

Let's recognize our charitable organizations as philanthropies — as existing from the Greek root which means "love for humankind."

Let's understand that our so-called independent organizations are dependently independent — dependent upon committed, concerned volunteers and on increasing income and estate resources to ensure — even to insure — our vital, indispensable philanthropies.

Key Obstacles to Board Effectiveness

The key obstacles to an involved, concerned, participatory governing board in terms of my experience are: 1) the absence of a written rationale for the existence and role of the board; 2) the absence of a studied design for the composition criteria, on-site/in-house orientation, and function of board members; and 3) the absence of management control and evaluation of the board and its members by the board itself, not the chairperson nor the chief executive officer.

What are the elements of management avoidance leading to these obstacles?

Obstacle #1. Preparation. Seldom, if ever, is the existence of a nonprofit organization's founding traced to the legal precedence of state not-for-profit corporate statutes. Therefore, governance managers and their appointed administrators serve in a functional vacuum in spite of the best of intentions.

Obstacle #2. Bylaws. The assumption exists that bylaws are the "law of operations." Bylaws are not law. At best they are mere management guidelines. And these guidelines change with every appointment of a new board chairperson and/or every new chief executive officer. Further, nine-tenths of all bylaws omit the basic provisions of existence — authority for existence under state not-for-profit corporate statutes; date and purpose of the articles of incorporation; date and approval of Internal Revenue Service approval of federal tax-exempt status; and recognition of founders.

Too many bylaws omit terms for board members; criteria for board membership; role and detailed function of standing committees; ad-hoc committees; honorary trustees; emeriti trustees; related councils; and replacement of the obsolete nomination committee by a small, crucial board management committee.

Obstacle #3. Budget. The organization governing board only considers the presented annual operating budget as resources necessary to "get by." Rarely does a board receive a proposed budget in terms of what resources are needed to ensure, even to insure, high-quality services. The difference represents a mission, service, and quality shortfall which accumulates faster and with greater negative impact than fiscal deficits. A balanced fiscal budget is no basis for jubilation unless the service deficit is also noted.

Obstacle #4. Board Design. Every governing board must have a design for membership numbers, characteristics desired, role, function, term, obligations, responsibilities, and personal/ joint accountability. Most boards should undergo a governance self study designed by and administered by an experienced nonprofit management consultant as a counsellor in philanthropy.

The design of a nonprofit governing board should be in the hands of the board management committee, which should consist of three persons, excluding the board chairperson as member or *ex officio* member. This committee must prescribe the personal characteristics desired of board members to ensure fulfillment of the mission of the organization. These characteristics include: kinds of talent, skills, experiences, professional and management roles, influence, affluence, proven wisdom and judgment, creative attitudes, and entrepreneurial goals. Underlying all of these is the evidence of constructive leadership as partnerships. Duplicative, as opposed to complementary, characteristics must be avoided.

Obstacle #5. Board Management. Generally the management of the nonprofit board of trustees falls in the crack between the board chairperson and the chief executive officer. (See page 184 for more on board management.)

Obstacle #6. Orientation. Seldom is a trustee who serves as a volunteer leader adequately prepared to serve in a public role as a dedicated advocate of the mission and services of the organization.

Upon a personal call for a candidate's consideration to serve as a trustee, the person should be presented with a **governing board manual** — a three-ring binder. This binder must include:

1. a relevant summary of the incorporating state's not-for-profit corporate statutes;
2. a copy of the articles of incorporation;
3. a copy of the state certification of approval;
4. a copy of the Internal Revenue Service letter of approval of 501(c)3 tax-exempt status;
5. a copy of the board-approved vision, mission, goals, and objectives of a long-term plan;
6. the description for the operation of a board of trustees;
7. the dated position description of a board of trustee member;
8. the dated position description of the chief executive officer;
9. a brief biography of each board member and the chief executive officer;
10. a detailed chart of the governing board and the organization;
11. an up-to-date copy of the bylaws as approved, dated, and signed by board officers; and
12. a chronological fact sheet plus facts of the last fiscal year.

Perhaps there is little more embarrassing or more useless for a newly appointed trustee than sitting in the office of the chief executive's office or board room for an "orientation" session. Here verbal descriptions of history, mission, plans, programs, personnel, and productivity stories just pass the newly appointed trustee by.

Rather, I suggest the **trustee-in-residence** plan which requires every new trustee to be on site for at least three days for an office-by-office, class-by-class, lab-by-lab, program-by-program observation as witness to live action.

A few years ago, upon suggesting this procedure to a board for newly appointed trustees, a regular, long-time trustee volunteered to be the first to spend a week on campus. She did. At the next board meeting she reported on her experience. She started out: "I have wasted 22 years of my life on this board because I never knew what all went on here. I visited every office, ate with students, ate with faculty on campus and at home, attended classes, attended meetings, and had my apartment open from seven to nine in the evening. As I was told, I never gave advice to anyone about anything. Now, I'm a whole new trustee." Everyone in the room had tears about her service grief. This is real, live action orientation.

Further, I suggest that every board and committee schedule a special *non-board member* visitor to report upon his or her profession, experience, and future expectancies all relevant to the mission of the organization. Such a presentation should not last more than half an hour.

Still further, I suggest that every board and committee schedule an **executive session** without any non-member in attendance. Here board members are alone — one-on-one — to raise questions, make suggestions, and discuss concerns all unrecorded. Trustees are seldom allowed to be alone. Staff executives are. Constituents are. But not trustees.

Given these data in advance of membership acceptance, the candidate will have a comprehensive perspective of what the organization is all about historically, currently, and in the short-term future at least.

Obstacle #7. Executive Committee. The original role of a governing board executive committee was designed to serve in the absence of the presence of the board and for emergency decisions. Even those decisions must be approved by the full board.

In the recent history of the independent sector, executive committees have become dominant in all, repeat all, board considerations and actions. Given this practice, all governing board members who are not members of the executive committee *must* resign their position as second-class trustees.

The executive committee role was never intended to replace, supplant, or denigrate the full board operation. The *entire* board of trustees is responsible under state law for all actions. No matter should be brought to the executive committee for action without having gone through a standing or special committee for study and recommendations to the full board, except for emergencies.

The executive committee must consist of all board officers and chairpersons of standing committees to assure committee study of important deliberations. The committee must meet only between regular board meetings and then upon call of the chairperson and the chief executive officer or three members of the committee.

Obstacle #8. Board Chairperson. Recently I was retained by a client to study and recommend changes in their governing board. The most sensitive problem was a man who served as board chairperson for 32 years. He was a very wealthy, highly respected person. He attended every meeting and every event. He liked people, especially those younger than him. He was a very, very modest donor. But no one wanted to challenge him because of his philanthropic potential (for which there was no evidence forthcoming).

In my report to the board for general reconstruction, I suggested the appointment of honorary trustees whom would be those who have never served as regular trustees. They are suggested because of their known leadership attributes to authenticate the humanitarian values of the organization.

When this long-time chairman heard the words (honorary trustee), he raised his hand and volunteered to be the first honorary trustee. The board members congratulated his voluntary action. Within three weeks all of my recommendations were in place with the notable exception of the one volunteer honorary trustee.

What should be the characteristics of a governing board chairperson?

First, chairpersons should have demonstrated leadership potential. Intangible though this criterion is, demonstration of leadership capacity is crucial in times of tension as well as when matters are routine. Those who are apathetic or apologetic for their role are as counterproductive as those who are dictatorial. The leadership of a board of trustees requires executive finesse, patience, humility, conviction and parliamentary skill, fairness, and concern for constructive board functions. The possession of leadership capacity is a talent; its use is a skill.

Second, chairpersons must be interested in, concerned for, understanding of, and students of nonprofits in all dynamics, demographics, and nuances.

Third, chairpersons must know their organization — its nature, its people, its programs, its problems, its potential. Only then can leadership talent and skills be inspirational and directive for the board and the entire constituency.

Fourth, chairpersons must interpret the forces and issues which may deter the organization from realizing fully its chartered purposes. They must prevent insulation or isolation from economic, political or demographic facts and changes in terms of interpreting organizational response *in advance* of a possible effect on the organization.

Fifth, chairpersons must possess strong intestinal fortitude. They must live with unpopular decisions, recalcitrant chief executive officers, loquacious trustees, difficult people — politicians, staff, faculty, parents, business leaders, associations, media personnel. Here is where fairness, respect, and understanding as personal attributes come into play but where spontaneous acquiescence has no role. The temptation to apply personal and official pressures abound. The chairperson serves only as a member of a board, not its chief authority. The chairperson is chair of the board as a whole, not its sole voice.

Sixth, chairpersons must respect and utilize the structure over which they are chairs. Policy consideration and policy making is for the board of trustees. Policies may be recommended by the administration or by the board. But the implementation of policy is the responsibility of the chief executive officer whom the board selects and evaluates. Trustee committee structure must be allowed to function for the study of policies, proposals, and evaluations and recommend accordingly. Short cuts, except in emergencies, frustrate the intent and practice of committee functions. Further, they in fact disenfranchise individual trustee responsibility and dissuade members from taking their role seriously.

Seventh, chairpersons must be managers and dreamers. They must manage their board and dream of what the board and organization may become in spite of evidence to the contrary. Most of the blame for the inability of boards of trustees to manage institutions stems from the inability of boards to manage their own destiny. Successful, dynamic, involved, concerned boards of trustees do not "just happen." Their validity and vitality results from conscious management direction. There is less research and study of trustee motivation and function than, perhaps, any other area of business or eleemosynary organizations. Yet, the responsibility of trustees to perform is firm, legal, and final.

Given these characteristics in abundance, how can a board chairperson better execute his/her leadership responsibility? One answer may be — very carefully. Here some guidelines may be of assistance. These result from my observations in all kinds of institutions with all kinds of problems. Some have implications of a general nature. Some are specific. All are intended to help chairpersons be better chairs.

The tenure of chairperson. Some believe that their appointment or election was by divine authority, hence, a life-long commitment to "fill the chair" results. Not so. The chairmanship is a human condition. When a person becomes convinced that he/she is indispensable as chair, both he/she and the organization are in trouble. A new chairperson must be concerned about the successor immediately. They must see to it that others on the board or those who are appointed or elected are of future chairperson quality insofar as this is possible. No person should remain as chair for more than five years. The contribution of time and talent usually is expended in terms of that particular role in five years' time. After this term, the chairperson deserves a new role. One-year terms do not compliment the holder, the organization or the public if the board or the organization takes the position of trustee chair seriously. The chairmanship should not become too comfortable, or too mechanical, or too inhibiting for promising new leadership. Society's rate of change in all sectors demands leadership renewal for validity, effectiveness, and societal relevance.

Chairperson and Chief Executive. How should a chairperson relate to the chief executive? Boss-employer? Buddy-buddy? Or protagonist-antagonist? None of these. First, one must try to understand chief executives. Some will say this is impossible. Perhaps so. But an attempt at understanding must be made. Many boards undertake the appointment of such executives with great seriousness, secrecy, and sacrosanct attitudes. Then, when the candidate accepts and reports, the board abdicates its responsibility and authority, allowing the chief executive "to run the darned thing." And so he or she does. They get to know the chairperson well if they can. If they can't, the chairperson of the selection committee soon becomes board chair. Then all is well for a while until something goes wrong or the chief executive is attracted elsewhere.

With this self-management function provided for, the chief executive and chairperson can assume a joint role of institutional leadership: one for policy consideration, adoption, and evaluation; the other for policy implementation. The role of each officer must be carefully delineated and mutually respected.

Know What a Board Can Be

Why trustees? Because of all they can give!

To give, not just to get. It is unconscionable that any person would desire or accept a nonprofit governing board position for personal gain — of ego, of position, of political favor, of financial benefit. To use the position for such purposes would be to misuse and abuse the integrity of the governing board and the ethics of the organization.

But to give what? Not all gifts are of equal value to the governing board, to the chief executive, or to the organization. Gifts of advice are valuable only in terms of the relevance of the advice given, how given, to whom given, and for what ulterior purpose. Most advice is cheap unless borne of empathetic understanding of the person to whom the advice is given or the situation requiring the advice.

Gifts of time are not of equal value. Loss of time is loss of individual commitment.

Give of your desire to be an involved, concerned, caring, participatory trustee.

Give of your time to listen, study, evaluate the dynamic demographics in our society affecting or likely to affect the organization.

Give of your time to become a trustee-in-residence to learn about the nature of the organization — its people, its staff, its programs and services, its constituents, its physical plant, its administrative functions.

Give of your time to know your fellow trustees.

Give of your home, church, and club to entertain people of the organization and its present and new friends.

Give of your advocacy for the organization on every possible occasion — for constituent recruitment, for enhancing the awareness of its distinction and for generous philanthropy.

Give of your personal resources to the fullest extent possible.

Give of your influence on others to join you in your concern for the essential nature of this special, free-enterprise, historic entity proudly, continuously, and profusely.

It is you to whom the public looks as authenticators of the validity of this humanitarian organization in serving present and future generations as it has served since its founding.

Prescription for an Effective Governing Board of a Not-for-Profit Organization

5 Imperatives for Organizational Success	5 Functions of the Board	5 Factors in Creating an Effective Board	Elements of Cost
1. Distinguished sponsorship	Authenticators of the organization	Assure satisfying experience	Advance candidate research
2. Relevant goals for future service	Serve as bridge for active advocacy	Match composition to leadership needs	Board design
3. Distinctive service record	Set policies to ensure quality	Inspire for positive decision making	Time and staff
4. Superior administration	Create and counsel administration	Evaluate effective operation	Shared responsibility
5. Progressive financing	Lead in resource development	Commitment to give and seek	Prospect research

When the prescription takes effect, there develops an acute sense of ownership, accountability, and responsibility resulting in deep personal pride and quiet fulfillment.

❧ 1 ❧
The Mission of Governance

Great governing boards of charitable organizations don't just happen; they must be designed for greatness, constantly tuned and honed.

Executive committees which "run" nonprofit organization governing boards relegate all other board members to second-class citizens. Second-class trustees should depart from "first-class" organizations.

For all that a board of trustees is not, there is much that it is. Becoming a trustee is a great honor, but the novelty wears off as the meetings wear on. To be an ineffective trustee is debilitating, but to be truly productive is exhilarating. Serving as an advocate, a salesperson, a leader for a worthy service organization unleashes personal potential — the trustee is not promoting himself or herself or selfish interests but can step forward as one who has already made a commitment and invites others to do so also: not on behalf of anyone, but for everyone.

Philanthropy Begins with Governance

In 1984, a most important book was published concerning why people give. It is called *Mega Gifts* (Bonus Books, Inc.,
1984). The author, Jerold Panas, interviewed 22 persons in
great depth and 19 gave him permission to use their names.
Each one had given more than one million dollars to charity.
Jerry, a distinguished philanthropic counsellor, wanted to know
why they did it. What were their criteria for sharing such
resources? He found out. The factors they cited are valid for
potential donors of any amount. This book stands as most
important for every governing board member, every officer,
and every resource development staff person.

These respondents look for evidence of confidence in the
possible application of their entrepreneurial talents, skills, experience, and potential of builders for greater and greater impact of
the organization's mission in an involuntary complex world.

These philanthropists first look to the governing board. Many
have served on nonprofit boards. They look to see who the board
is; evidence of management perspectives such as the appointment
of competent executives; fiscal stability of the organization; the
elimination of all debt; and evidence of fulfillment of the mission
and goals of the organization.

Successful philanthropy, at whatever level, depends upon the
art of human motivation. That motivation starts with governance — not needs, not tax consequences, not fancy publications.
Governance means "the art, manner, function or power of government" (Webster's New World Dictionary). Motivation means
inciting from apathy to caring to sharing to investing.

Nonprofit organizations are *managed* by their board of
governance. They are *administered* by a board-appointed chief
executive.

These basics are conditions preceding the motivation for
continuous and generous philanthropy:

1. reasons for having a governing board beyond the
   number required for founding the organization under
   auspices of the articles of incorporation;

2. position description of board membership including all personal responsibilities, obligations, and functions;
3. criteria for membership including talent, skill, wisdom, judgment, and experience needed by the organization in fulfillment of stated purposes, mission, goals, objectives, and policies of the organization; and,
4. provisions for governing board management and evaluation of membership, role, and function by a board management committee replacing the obsolete nominating committee.

Confidence must be built by designing an ideal governing board of persons of influence and affluence as well as representativeness; designing the ideal position of chief executive officer, finding, helping, evaluating, and/or relieving that person; and designing a comprehensive plan for the future requiring diverse resources for fiscal stability.

One by-product of these strategies should be a comprehensive resource development program. This should include private sector funds to guarantee balanced budgets; urgent, non-deferrable personnel, program, and physical plant requirements; urgent, but deferrable requirements; and an untotalled tabulation of endowment investment gift opportunities. Herein lies a philanthropic marketing plan for prospective donor consideration for gifts from income for the organization's income plus bequest and estate plan considerations attributable to some one to five percent of the constituents.

Today, asset-building funds are sought and come from diverse personal resource assets of a small number of constituents who hold or who can create or release diverse assets for special interest objectives.

Nearly 90 percent of all funds given are given by individuals, couples, families; 10 percent by businesses and foundations. Ideally, then, 90 percent of staff and volunteer time and 90 percent of budget expense should be devoted to the one to five percent of the constituents who can have great impact on the organization philanthropically. This concentration of effort requires personnel of great, great human relations sensitivity and great creative talent in the identification, cultivation, solicitation, and follow-up skills. Here again, the book *Mega Gifts* can be a guide for unprecedented philanthropic productivity.

In these remarks I have concentrated upon two major management factors:

1. Positioning — setting forth the management conditions preceding the philanthropic productivity expected, earned and deserved; and
2. Marketing — by designing the destiny of the organization through comprehensive planning which results in diverse resource support for diverse objectives available from individuals, families, businesses, foundations, and associations. (See appendix F, page 231.)

Seldom is generous philanthropy an accident. Generosity, too, must be earned and deserved and its roots — its tap root — is confidence in management.

Perspectives on Trusteeship

Individuals are not born to be trustees, to hold and be responsible for the management of our cultural, social, health, educational, religious or other prized organizations particular to our democracy. Organizations are formed to meet the needs of the trustees' humanitarian role. Therefore, two disparate entities must seek and find a mutuality of interest and concern leading to respect and understanding of the roles of each other in one common purpose.

None of our institutions are immortal simply because they happen to exist in our presence.

Destiny must be designed and earned as a conscious, consistent commitment to serving humankind's needs. This is the spiritual nature of philanthropy — the giving of one's resources, be they time, talent or treasure — current, capital or perpetual.

Those historic organizations no longer in existence were governed by nice people who managed their demise. Leadership is a real factor. Not domination. Persuasive, creative, concerned leadership.

Unless membership criteria and characteristics exist and unless those features reflect the qualities necessary for serving the particular nature of the organization's services, the board membership search is at sea aimlessly bouncing about, subject to variable winds and whims.

Here, then, are the basic building blocks for rebuilding a governing board. Not confronting these factors squarely is the same as applying Band-Aids to terminal management ills.

There is an art in dealing with the diverse, sensitive human factors in governing board relationships. But above and far beyond must be the consideration of the worth of the organization governed. These questions must be answered:

1. Would this organization be missed if it didn't exist? Really? By whom?
2. Who is performing or could perform our services better? By our closure? Merger?
3. Where should we be in five years? Ten years? Twenty-five years?
4. What are our costs and assets required for fiscal stability?

To exist or to govern merely to sustain mediocrity in personnel, in services, in equipment, in facilities provides no cause for inspiration, aspiration or true credibility. Society can be saved harassment by the demise of many of our so-called charitable organizations. Perhaps their greatest charitable act would be to cease operations, having fulfilled their mission on a quality basis. No student in America has been denied a college education by the demise of some 400–500 colleges since 1970. What they have been denied is a mediocre education.

Governing boards must assess what they are governing, to what societal purpose. Governing boards should not be an organizational appendage. The pain of surgery usually restores to wholeness and greater health the ills of mankind. Why not, then, with our organizations in need of greater leadership, physical, fiscal, and service benefits for mankind? The stress of today's economy is the most opportune time for total reevaluation of all our voluntary resources. Again and finally, mere existence is not a right either for immortality of organizations or members of governing boards.

The name of the game in board membership is power, not representativeness nor nice, friendly people. Power to do. Power to influence. Power to advocate. Power to lead. Power to communicate to others the organization's validity, service, and fiscal requirements.

The future of nonprofit organizations requires a massive change in attitudes toward proclaiming the positive worth of each of our humanitarian organizations. Issues of confidence in what has been, what is, and what is to be stimulates motivation of unprecedented leadership and both motivation and inspiration to concentrate upon achieving numbers of dollar investments from donor investors not just numbers of donors.

There are new challenges for new board leadership:

1. the impact of high technology can hardly be imagined but it's here;
2. much of what has been written and preached about trusteeship is obsolete;
3. fewer members of a board will assure higher productivity;
4. a high number of members is an obsolete goal;
5. concentrate upon asset-building not fund raising;
6. prepare to endow out of the budget all features to make room for non-budgeted requirements;
7. many organizations will cease to exist because of adding large numbers of board members, not emphasizing leadership requirements, counting upon obsolete resource development personnel, and reducing the existence of redundant organization programs and services; and
8. organizations will initiate programs to set their "worth" to insure their future through generous philanthropy.

Leadership in Action

Leadership — the word, the position, the title — is a fragile, intangible term applied to conscience assumed, expressed, or expected.

Leadership is an innate talent lying dormant until expressed voluntarily or involuntarily. The leadership attributed to tsars, dictators, tyrants — whether political, commercial, civic, religious, social — are voluntary assumptions of power by virtue of office irrespective of humane interdictions.

Involuntary leadership occurs at times of instantaneous tragedy affecting humankind. When an average person is confronted by some force affecting human life or actions affecting human comfort, that person's immediate response to help is dramatic, dynamic involuntary leadership.

Leadership is sometimes applied in a systematic, progressive, inspirational manner or, in times of dramatic stress, applied instantaneously.

Leaders are not born to lead. Leadership cannot be learned from books or study of others. Followers can become leaders given the occasion to express themselves for others. Leaders respond to the urgency and necessity to lead when others are not yet ready to assert themselves. Leaders possess a definite sense of ego which is sometimes mild, even suppressed; others are egomaniacs and become irresponsible dictators confronting all evidence of rationality.

Model leaders create a purpose in their leadership role:

- to accomplish a mission, set definite and measurable goals from studied demographics, plans, and wise counsel;
- to anticipate and prepare for obstacles deterring steady, positive progress;
- to develop initiatives in creative points of measurable growth;
- to take risks and learn from them lessons on how to meet and capitalize upon new risks;

- to communicate ideas, ideals, vision, and dreams to others in persuasive ways for them to join in the growth process;
- to listen by active hearing, not prejudging results;
- to encourage trust, confidence, reliability among those who are vital to progress;
- to unlock the locked; dream the impossible; accomplish the unprecedented in sequential steps; and
- to explain, teach, develop a process, understand others and show them the way.

There are always obstacles to effective leadership, from prejudice to egocentrism; from crises to tragedies; from size dimensions to diverse complexities; from time limits to constraints of followers; and from inadequate resources to unprepared environments.

Leaders prepare for obstacles through undiscovered talent and skills. They learn from listening, from observing, from persuading, from moving forward, from communication — never retreating nor parking. This interplay creates unexpected leadership, progress, history in unexpected dimensions.

Persons who are never tried, never lead.

Board Responsibilities for Procurement of Resources

Perhaps the single greatest matter of concern before policy boards, officers, and administrators today is the question of financing the ongoing operation of the organization, whether educational, cultural, healthcare, religious, social, or other. The changing modes of administration all have financial implications.

Notable experts have authored numerous works on the subject of financing nonprofit human services. Study groups, commissions, task forces, conferences, bureaus, centers of research, consortia each and all add to the thinking, if not the knowledge, of the problem and the opportunities for resolution. Regardless of this tide of talk and printer ink, the solutions for each organization cannot be found solely in external resources. Rather, solutions must be discovered internally first. Within the human characteristics of ingenuity and perspicacity of the organization's leadership, study, and concern can discover new and flexible alternatives.

Policy boards hold dual responsibility. *First,* policy boards have ultimate, non-transferable responsibility for the procurement of essential financial resources. No other body is responsible by law for the management of the organization regardless of how a board may wish to delegate or abdicate this function. *Second,* boards have responsibility for determining, as objectively as is humanly possible, the degree of wisdom by which existing resources are managed. In seeking to meet that responsibility, each policy board member must ask herself or himself a profound, personal, moral question — does this organization deserve to survive? Or, if this organization ceased to exist, who would miss it? Again, mere existence is insufficient rationale for forced survival.

Responsibility for resource procurement must be preceded by absolute assurance that all measures for the conservation and utilization of existing resources are maximized. Our way of life is challenged in every direction. The risks of luxury must be balanced against the costs of necessity and proof of utility. Deep concerns mandate thoughtful, studied actions. Policy boards must be assured of absolute needs through honest, thorough staff preparation for clear background documentation leading to tough, impersonal decision-making.

In this age of uncertainty there are no shortcuts to fiscal viability. Boards will be called upon to make difficult, unpopular decisions. Before those decisions are made, the board has a right to expect of itself and its associates within the organization careful consideration of certain essential preconditions. Implementation of these preconditions will strengthen the confidence in management as it seeks to prove that it has earned the support it seeks. In summary form, there are nine preconditions for fiscal procurement responsibility whether from private or public sources or both.

Responsibility #1. Response. Not Reaction. As a general observation, policy boards just simply do not provide themselves ample opportunity to discuss among themselves informally or thoroughly economic, social, and demographic forces, issues, trends, and data as these apply to their organization. In the hustle and bustle of getting through agenda, real issues and constraints which may be analyzed in open discussion are seldom confronted. To the extent humanly possible, all pressures and strains that may be felt by the organization must be anticipated in advance, studied, analyzed, and weighed in terms of programmatic, human, and fiscal impact. Only then can viable options for choice be identified and evaluated.

One public university found itself in increasing disfavor with new legislators, whereas for decades before the institution was favored and received more than adequate financing. Someone forgot to analyze the nature of the composition of the legislature. No longer were its members farmers. Suddenly they were attorneys — not specific beneficiaries of the institution's services.

Boards and organizations must plan for flexibility to be responsive rather than reactive. In too many cases, crisis plans and crisis budgets have become standard practice. Too many boards are satisfied to be custodians of the status quo. Some are insulated or isolated from the reality of present or future dangers. Some are inundated by so much paper that major issues remain vague or hidden. Some boards are apathetic enough to "let George worry about it." George is usually the chief executive officer. Most boards do not schedule the time or the occasion to talk as board members among themselves about the tangible and intangible probabilities threatening or likely to affect present comfort.

Board members have no excuse for being less than totally informed about the organization they hold in public trust. They have the right and the obligation to require the chairman, chief executive officer, and senior staff to keep them informed of current and projected problems and opportunities. No less important should be the efforts by every member of the board to initiate learning about key issues and forces that will affect that trust, input which should come from organizations such as professional associations and from personal reading, study, and reflection.

Some acute observers of the modern scene hold that societal change is now occurring in 90-day cycles. Even if this judgment is somewhat extreme, it is clearly not too soon to anticipate impending problems as we know them.

Thus boards and executive officers have an inescapable joint responsibility to share information and concern for what will be, not only for what is. In this connection, can you recall the agenda from your last board meeting? Did it follow Parkinson's Law of Triviality? ". . . The time spent on any item on an agenda will be in inverse proportion to the sum involved." You need only insert other words for "sum" like "policy importance."

Preparation for the future begins with the guardians of that future who are responsible in law for the management of institutions — an obligation calling for no less and perhaps more personal integrity than one can be expected to exercise in the management of one's own business or personal life.

Responsibility #2. The Chief Executive. Policy boards must assure and reassure themselves that they have the best possible chief executive. This is not the time for the board to rest in idle self-assurance that "we have a nice CEO or COO." Nice executives finish last with nice organizations.

Such executives should be *management irritants* to their boards. They must assiduously educate board members objectively and persistently about present and future issues as they see them and in realistic, honest, even harsh terms. Too often, relationships to boards are at least tolerant; at worst feudal. Too often, more effort is expended to protect turf than in motivating and facilitating dedicated, invaluable, wise decision-making by boards in control.

Yet, great tribute and honor must go to those officers whose leadership and art of management far exceed public knowledge. Their developed skills in managing the internal affairs of program, services, facilities, volunteers, and staff for ever greater relevancy and utilization in the face of great odds too often goes unstated and unrewarded. We are heartened by the remarkable ingenuity of some administrators in devising processes, methods, and means for assuring quality in program innovation, research, and service. Policy boards are generally unaware of these attributes of officers and staff within their own organization. This makes it most difficult to identify and reward constructive change and penalize the opposite.

Responsibility #3. Deficits. Policy boards must assure themselves that their institution has a valid, objective, studied vision of the future and a master plan that is continually updated. Without such a plan, how is it possible for boards to evaluate adopted policies, review and relate financial requests, analyze the effectiveness of services, and approve financial programs? Without this knowledge, previously planned and approved programs and services cannot be related to proposed budgets, leaving boards unaware of the risks of a programmatic deficit even before the consideration of financial deficits. The operating divisions through policy board committees should present their budgets on what it really should cost to provide advertised objectives. Then boards can decide what they must "settle for" in both budgets.

The necessity to secure resources must first depend upon what programs and services the organization is seeking to offer its constituency. These activities should be the first concerns of board programmatic committees. Instead, we find most of these committees the least active, least informed, and least concerned of all board committees. Yet, in their hands rest the issues of purpose and functions that in the end will determine the organization's future. The program committee should be responsible for the master plan and all of its elements, including the preparation of a budget of necessity at the same time others are preparing financial budgets. They should be prepared to respond to alternative options and examine proposed changes in terms of costs and risks on behalf of quality education, student services, and public services. Only with such input from the board level can finance committees operate effectively and comprehend projected costs and benefits. In short, finance committees should not set program policy, but without projected programmatic budgets there is no alternative.

Responsibility #4. Management Assurance. Policy boards have a right to assure themselves of effective and efficient programs through the retention of specialists.

Most organizations have outstandingly competent staff who, through the CEO, serve the board and the organization with great concern and dedication. But boards can only delegate authority, not responsibility, for management. Seldom do boards seek objective assurance that the organization is well managed.

Most boards rest on prepared statements by staff officers, all of which are self-congratulatory, seldom self-immolating. One institution recently adopted the following bylaw, which I recommend as consistent with board responsibility. It should be an example for all organizations:

Periodic Review of the Organization. To assure that every aspect of the management and operations of the organization is being performed with due effectiveness and within the general policies laid down by the Board, there shall be conducted a periodic audit and review of the state of the organization, emphasizing progress toward major goals and objectives. At least once every five years there shall be an evaluation of: (1) the general management of the organization with special reference to the Office of the Chief Executive Officer and the chief administrative offices; (2) the mission's services; (3) the business affairs, physical plant, and grounds management; (4) the programs for public relations, resource development, and financing; and (5) the Board operation and trustee member effectiveness. The review and evaluation shall be conducted or authorized by the Board as it deems appropriate and reported to the full Board. Trustees and Board committees shall be involved as appointed or directed by the Chairman of the Board following consultation with the Chief Executive Officer.

Corporate boards and government agencies surround themselves constantly with the best possible advice to assure that the decision-making process selects the most promising of all possible options. A policy board taking such steps complements the chief executive and the senior staff and validates standard or special operating procedures.

Attempts by well-meaning board members to loan otherwise able management executives, who are inexperienced in the human and procedural nuances of nonprofit organizations, can be painfully counterproductive and are seldom beneficial.

Instead, resource persons of proven competence and effectiveness in the related field and in the matter under consideration should be made available to the board, its committees, and the senior management staff as appropriate.

Responsibility #5. Financial Options. Shifting resource bases require constant alertness and interpretation. No one can rest assured that present sources are permanently certain. The relationships and impact of service costs and fee changes, gift and grant commitments and expectancies, investment income, auxiliary enterprises, collateral enterprises, and public sector support are tender variables subject to both consumer response and public policy.

Large organizations usually have experienced, trained planning specialists constantly studying options, models, statistics, and demographic impact. Small organizations must rely upon commercial/research/professional specialists to analyze and project their options. Some associations offer this valuable service. To rely upon professionals who are members of the board, sometimes for free or reduced cost services, immediately activates ethical conflict of interest problems.

Financial managers, business officers, and finance committees have a most arduous responsibility as strategists on economic policy and market trends. While new resources are being created, whether in the public sector or the private sector, alternate options must include plans for major exigencies with financial implications.

Responsibility #6. Staff Ingenuity. Policy boards must be assured that staff capabilities, programs, and procedures exist to maximize potential financial response from constituents, whether beneficiary constituents; local, state or federal governments; businesses or foundations.

Publicly assisted organizations, faced with sharing priority allocations of public funds to meet other social concerns, have found the private sector to be responsive. Private sector support to these organizations increases each year. Why? Because constituents were asked for support in substantial terms, which they always provided.

One community college district had over two million alumni, mostly within its geographic region, over 75 percent of whom did not seek further higher education. This constituency literally was overlooked for both financial and other support purposes.

Similarly, independent organizations found the public sector resources to be responsive to their historic, unheralded, and substantial services to the public at large. These institutions found that they had a highly motivational case which councilmen, commissioners, assemblymen, and legislators could no longer ignore.

In the past five years, many states have developed formulae to substantially assist independent organizations. Such allocations may increase.

The exploration of support markets and constituencies is not a business-as-usual process for relations or development office personnel. Organizational affairs today require experienced, sophisticated executives far beyond heretofore traditional capacities.

Responsibility #7. Constituent Perceptions. Different organizations view their prime constituents through different eyes. It is increasingly clear that economic necessity is forcing the exercise of options, heretofore unexplored, to seek and obtain financial support to assure survival, if not to guarantee quality performance. For independent organizations, the public sector is now being "accommodated." For public organizations, the private sector is a rich target for "new money."

1. *Independent Institutions.* Policy boards must be assured that public sector leadership — those who are invisible as well as those who are visible — are recognized and treated as a distinct constituency. A special program of education, communication, involvement, and action can be created and implemented for key political leaders as well as for program participants, patients, members, alumni, parents and families, civic leaders, church leaders, businesspeople, and foundation leaders. These organizations must be careful that annual or special fund support requested is consistent with the motivational case for support and in terms of the capacity of the resource, whether public bodies or individual prospective donors.

2. *Church-Related Institutions.* Policy boards are often chiefly ecclesiastical, quite introspective, and suspicious of generous financial support from both public and private sectors lest some of their "power" or "control" be jeopardized. Yet, perhaps the greatest deterrence lies with the provincial or parochial mentality unwilling to consider and adopt policy guidelines

to preserve ideals, concepts, or control preferences. Such boards must be cognizant of risks for survival and risks of *professions of quality and service; without strong counterbalancing programs of outstanding leadership enlistment, recruitment of outstanding chief executives, and obtaining outstanding support from church constituents as well as public constituents will be difficult.* Here the management exigencies are far more complex, less statistical, more emotional, and less motivational to the public generally.

Responsibility #8. Tax Implications. There is much discussion of tax reform measures at all government levels. No one is against tax reform per se. Yet, under the guise of the label appears an insidious attempt to nationalize nonprofits contrary to our heritage of self-determination of rights and privileges. The prospect of severe curtailment of philanthropic gift procedures, while aimed at "the rich," affects in far greater measure middle class citizens who are modest stockholders and holders of real property assets. Too, it is obvious from massive federal assistance programs that federal distribution of funds really benefits most those who are hired to distribute such funds — not the average recipient of services nor the institutions providing such services.

Already personal estate tax provisions are substantially confiscatory when federal and state provisions are applied. Powerful, positive, aggressive programs and actions must be implemented to offset misrepresented benefits of tax deprivation parading as tax reform.

Each board member should participate in advocating her or his personal and/or organizational views with positive, politically persuasive arguments for retention of present gift and estate tax provisions. Each fiscal year, people — individuals like you and me — give 89 percent of the total funds given voluntarily. Of that percentage, about six percent is by bequest. Even if these procedures are maintained, policy boards should press for aggressive planned giving programs that concentrate on bequest and estate plan provisions as well as gifts of appreciated assets.

Responsibility #9. Organizational Marketing. Policy boards must be aware of the marketing credentials of their organization for beneficiary constituents, public support, and/or private support in new terms. Consumers of nonprofit organization services have become wise to economic benefits as well as service benefits of largeness versus smallness and new approaches to the process versus the traditional lecture. Public relations efforts which have been tried and true now require a new sensitivity in terms of: motivating essential values not just traditions; cost-benefit ratios not just habits; stimulating experiences in diverse services interchange; services for young and old; and taking services to where the need is.

The interpretative strategy and tactics demand new expertise, new skills which very few organizations are prepared to acknowledge. Yet, at every turn we find that we are not in a business-as-usual society or environment. All organizations must market themselves in new terms to new and old constituents in new ways to demonstrate that they have earned and are earning greater financial support from all sectors.

Summary: What is being asked, what you must ask yourselves, individually and collectively, is whether your stewardship of our organizations of human services merit the investment of increasing amounts of social resources?

Your greatest challenge and your finest opportunity for service to society and fulfillment of your own noblest ideals rests upon your ability and willingness to face this question honestly and fearlessly. How you respond to this call may well determine the future course of our indispensable nonprofit organizations, which in turn will have major impact on the future of our country and the world.

The Chief Executive Officer Search

Our society today, indeed our nation and the world, are subject to two gigantic forces of which we can only absorb small dimensions. One such force is the changing technology and social dynamics; the second is the changing demographics. What is is not what will be, but we do not know when.

The historic, proud tradition of neighbor caring for neighbor, community caring for community, and the not-for-profit organization standing as the pillar of voluntary caring for humanitarian cultural, educational, health, and civic services appears threatened. The value-centered services of our democracy today demand unprecedented entrepreneurship to overcome the satisfactions of status quoism exemplified by both governance and administration.

The tendency to survive, not thrive toward fiscal stability and security requires new dimensions of management and administrative partnership. Our information society dominates our past manufacturing world dominance. Our multinational interventions are of enormous dimensions. Our comfort in anticipating public sector support "to get by" is no longer assured.

The statistics and projections of changes in our society are startling, as if the undergirding rug of comfort is being withdrawn to erode our conviction of what is, what shall be and be forever. Not so. The composition of our community has already changed substantially. So have the values of those changes. The values we have cherished will be secured, even insured, by limited constituents — the power of the present private sector.

The "authentic board of trustees" must lie somewhere between the three-person board of smaller nonprofits and a 106-member board of a state university. Then there was a hospital with 28 board members and 103 three-person committees among those 28 persons!

In my role since 1948 as a philanthropic management counsellor, I have become preoccupied with giving *a priori* attention to management preconditions for fund program success. Increasingly, individuals, businesses, foundations, organizations, and agencies give major attention in seeking evidence of confidence in the requesting organization beginning with *who* is the governing board.

The authentic board must be designed to be authentic and not just a happenstance of friends inviting friends for a comfortable ego position. Trusteeship today is awesomely serious business for interested, concerned, committed, caring persons. More joiners are unwelcome.

The alpha and the omega of the chief executive search process is the fact that the governing board selects, manages, and dismisses the chief executive officer of the organization they hold as a public trust. Any persons or any bodies from whom representatives are sought to join in the search process can be no more than advisory to the governing board. There is no basis in concept or in fact that the chief executive officer has or must have *a priori* academic approval any more than he or she must be an accountant, an architect, a salesperson, an investment specialist or other "representative" of a particular organization function. The chief executive must be many things to many constituencies simultaneously. Unless the governing body accepts this principle, the governing body is abdicating a responsibility or delegating an authority which cannot be delegated or both.

In creating the chief executive search committee, the governing board must select from among its members three to five persons believed to be, in practice, the most sensitive, intuitive, perceptive, and able judges of executive talent possible. Also, they must be especially adept at meeting with and dealing with representative members of constituent groups, never flaunting their *a priori,* residual, and ultimate authority in the process.

The governing board resolution creating the chief executive search committee should also recommend the composition of the committee, authorize the retention of special counsel, approve a budget, and cite that no more than five candidates be recommended from the committee to the governing board for their ultimate decision. And then, the governing board individually and collectively must maintain a "hands off" policy until recommendations are made (unless a crisis in the management of the committee occurs).

After the committee is formed, the chairperson must make clear that, with the seating of the committee, all representation stops mandating that the committee function is to identify candidates for the organization as a whole — not a particular group. Persons unable to meet this mandate must relinquish their position at this point and proceed no further with the committee. Further, the chairperson must admonish that every process, every meeting, every discussion, every piece of paper, every observation is absolutely confidential, privileged information available only to the committee and to no one else.

The chairperson, to further assure absolute confidentiality of all elements of the process, must select a committee secretary/ stenographer. It is preferable that the person not be an employee of the organization. All pertinent records must be kept in locked files with two keys only; one for the secretary, one for the chairperson. A separate mailing location is preferable for the receipt of all mail for the committee.

The committee, when formed and ready to function, should have a general agenda somewhat as follows:

1. Who or what or where or why is our organization? Why would anyone want to be CEO of our organization? The committee itself must discuss and answer these questions. Also, they must be ready to answer these and many, many more questions from chief executive candidates themselves. Remember, the candidate most desired as CEO will be "selecting" the organization more assiduously than the committee will probably be "selecting" him or her. What does the charter say? The bylaws? Policy, trustee, staff, administrative manuals and other key documents? How shall we present (or represent) our organization? All of this should result in the preparation of a key document — more than a fact sheet — a case for the organization in brief form. Persuasive, honest, complete problems must be cited — financial, leadership, academic/ professional recruitment, board leadership role, and function, etc. Of course, it should not be distributed except to legitimate candidates.

2. What is expected of a CEO, say, in the next five years? Ten years? Builder or custodian? Extrovert or introvert? Sales personality or laboratory researcher? Advocate or adversary? Negotiator? Leader? Creative? Open? Fund raiser? Manager? Social? Traveler? Family? Politician? Someone to fill a chair or create an aura? Someone who loves people, opens new markets for constituents and programs?

3. What should be reasonable criteria and qualifications for candidates given resolution of questions #1 and #2 above? What

about those crucial factors not appearing in credentials or from references? Who will judge management style, sense of self-worth, how he/she helps people grow, intuition, true dimensions of past successes, one who has honest doubts, a sense of humor, one who can laugh at himself/herself? How shall these criteria be presented, discussed, and evaluated?

4. Create a board-approved chief executive position description. Realistic. Genuine. Task-oriented. Goal-oriented. Problem-oriented. Or, an artful combination of these. It must be carefully prepared.

5. Announcement of vacancy. Set a deadline for receipt of nominations and applications. Nominations are not acceptable without a comprehensive statement as to why the person is nominated. The announcement should be in local, area, national, and special publications that are sent to area organizations and parents of constituents, faculty/professional administrators, friends of the organization, special donors, selected businesses, and foundations. Never seek "also rans" from other institution selection processes.

6. Set up a process for receiving, recording, and responding immediately to all letters. Avoid trite, curt, mechanical responses. Anticipate follow-up letters to all nominators and other helpful persons at the conclusion of the process either before or after the public announcement of appointment.

7. Set up a process for reviewing credentials and required documentation before committee evaluation. Provide standardized forms for evaluation of documentation plus a system for grading: A — top qualifications; B — good, but must see; C — appears to be some doubt; D — not a candidate (state reason).

8. Provide an opportunity for each member of the committee to see each candidate's credentials for assurance that prejudices and other factors are avoided and to assure each nominee or applicant that the record in hand was evaluated. At evaluation sessions present, evaluate, and eliminate lower categories with reasons for such decisions in writing and filed for confidentiality. Discuss promising candidates, credentials, nominators, references.

9. Advise suspended candidates immediately and gracefully.

10. Request top candidates to supply additional information as to perceptions of the CEO office or elements of the position.

Contact references including stamped return envelope with prepared questions relative to the candidate being researched.

11. When the evaluation process gets down to five or 10 candidates, the handling process becomes sensitive. The chairperson should telephone or write to advise the candidate as soon as possible to learn if the candidacy is still valid.

12. Candidates are usually invited to the organization site alone to meet with the committee, officers, staff, and constituents. Allowance must be made for free time of the candidate to tour and to wander through the physical plant at will. After each candidate visit, one person should "collect" impressions and evaluations before the appearance of the next candidate.

13. After all candidates have appeared, the committee should meet to further arrive at a determination of those who should be among the top candidates, whose spouse should be invited to join the candidate on another visit. A careful agenda should be outlined to make the joint appearance as comfortable as possible.

14. After these visits, the committee should determine the top three candidates and prepare their recommendations for the board of trustees.

15. The committee should meet with appropriate organization officers concerning the public announcement process.

At the initiation of the CEO search process, a determination should be made as to the selection of experienced counsel to assist the committee. The role of counsel is that of accelerating the process, the prevention of unintended mistakes and recommendations of optional procedures. Counsel must not be used to interview or contact candidates. Experience has demonstrated that, when this happens, desirable candidates are turned off assuming that the search committee has abdicated its special responsibility. When the process is delegated to professional "head hunters," the process has to be mechanical, not representing the organization first by those in and of it rather than those just at it. Special chief executive search counsel can become very valuable in contacting associates of the top candidates at their present location to ascertain personal management style, nuances, eccentricities, etc., about which the committee should know in advance and confidentially.

At the conclusion of the process, a synopsis of the process should be prepared "for the record" and the correspondence, rating, etc., should be destroyed. The committee must turn over all records to the chairperson for destruction.

The governing board should invite the search committee to the announcement session as a courtesy and for expression of appreciation.

Position Description of a Not-for-Profit Organization Governing Board

Volunteer members of governing boards have functional responsibilities, accountability, and obligations as do paid staff members of the organizations they govern. In fact, governing board members have both legal and fiduciary responsibilities even though they are volunteers. While the position is one of honor and respect, expectancy for accountability is evermore awesome because of involuntary economic and social forces, issues, and trends. These factors alone encourage a strong partnership between the governing board and chief executive officer to assure programmatic, service, and fiscal management requirements for a certain destiny of stability and security and mission fulfillment.

Responsibility. First, each governing board and each nonprofit corporation functions under the authority of legislated statutes which exist in every state to assure that the organization operates in the best interests of the people of the state in which the organization is incorporated. While the governing board has both authority and responsibility to function as the articles of incorporation stipulate, the governing board may delegate *authority* to function to a chief executive officer but cannot delegate its ultimate *responsibility*.

Second, to mandate state authority to function according to the approved articles of incorporation.

Third, bylaws serve only as management guidelines for the systematic implementation of state statutes and articles of incorporation. The bylaws must provide governing board members specifics of functions as a *standard of management* and requirements to serve society, to assure the mission, and to perform stated services. Bylaws which are merely schematic operational guidelines do not provide sincere and dedicated individuals the satisfactions for specific functional expectancies of personal or official duties.

Role. Trustees are policy makers not policy implementers. Trustees retain, evaluate, and replace policy implementers who are chief executive officers. Trustees hold the organization in trust and must assure efficient and effective management of services, programs, personnel, plant, and finance requirements for the mission and goals. They must plan for the organization's future; they must design its destiny from all standpoints — from assessment of external forces to reexamination of the validity of internal services. Their leadership expectations for others must begin with themselves in public demonstration for others to follow. This exemplary leadership includes active public advocacy, participation in organization functions and personal financial support.

Criteria. Individual candidates must possess the personal attributes of talents, skills, and experience needed by the organization to accomplish the approved mission, goals, and plans. In addition, each person must possess the elusive characteristics of unprejudiced objectivity, wisdom, and judgment to assess all proposed policy and evaluation considerations.

While each board must consist of a spectrum and balance of social, civic, professional, economic, business, constituency and other representatives relevant to the nature of the organization, the point at which representativeness ceases is when board or committee meetings are called to order. Then and there each trustee is a single, joint representative as a trust officer of the organization to which he or she was elected.

Each trustee nominee is expected to become a student of the organization which the trustee is expected to govern. The trustee is expected to set aside time to serve as a responsible, responsive, caring, involved, concerned trustee. Reports, proposals, analyses, publications, minutes, and past policies must be studied, analyzed, and contemplated in advance of decision-making.

Management. Trustees should expect to be managed by their own board management committee and staffed by the organization's chief executive officer. From orientation as a new trustee, each board member serves in a management/governance partnership of constant attention to all features and functions of the board's operations.

The trustees should expect that all major issues shall be considered by appropriate standing committees first and not by the executive committee except in emergency situations. If executive committees begin to make all decisions and merely report these to the board, non-executive committee members should resign their second-class positions and avoid statutory legal and financial responsibilities. Trustees — effective, concerned trustees — are made, not born.

Abuse. Individuals abuse their position and role as trustees:

1. when they arrive at the point where they determine that their position is a divine right and remain as a board member too long;
2. when they bring prejudices into official decision-making;
3. when they decline to make generous personal contributions to the full extent of their capacity, thereby helping to meet gaps in budgets they approve;
4. when they entertain complaints or other contacts from those serving under the chief executive officer thereby violating channels of communication;
5. when they find themselves unable to give a public address on behalf of the organization they govern because they are unfamiliar with its mission, its people, programs, services, and its future potential;
6. when they are unprepared to make wise decisions because of not setting aside time to study the issues, implications, and alternatives;
7. when they represent conflicts of interest thereby protecting personal or family or business self-gain;
8. when they interfere with administrators in the implementation of policies and administrative procedures;
9. when they press for special privilege for family or friends;
10. when they miss too many meetings for whatever reasons and fail to resign;
11. when they assume positions of ultra-conservatism which they would not tolerate in their own businesses, professions, or lifestyle thereby constraining organizational stability and security;

12. when they cannot respect confidences when confidences are requested; and
13. when they accept the trustee position in lieu of payment for services rendered.

Trustees are human. Many are misled as to why they are selected as candidates and what is expected of them when asked for their agreement to be nominated. The trustee's position is at once fragile and powerful. The honor of selection must not blind the individual to the tender complexities involved in merely saying, "yes." (See appendix H, page 235.)

Criteria for Trustee
Candidate Consideration

As the board management committee considers nominees for board membership, each individual must consider in light of the following questions who would be the best candidate to round out the predetermined essential characteristics needed among individual board leadership and confidential building strengths of the board:

1. Suitability as a Trustee

- Will he/she fulfill an important role on the board?
- Will his/her membership on the board contribute to the rounding out of the total trustee complex of strengths, abilities, and experience necessary for policy direction?
- Does he/she possess a degree of competence and experience needed on the board?
- Is he/she in a position of influence with others who are important to the success of the organization? Is he/she likely to use that influence?

2. General Preparation as a Trustee

- Has he/she been briefed on the problems, plans, and potential for the organization?
- Does he/she know the organization's history, philosophy, and plans and will he/she endeavor to keep abreast of relevant national trends?
- Does he/she understand functions of trustees — to establish and guide policy, establish effective management, keep out of administration, and assist in the organization's growth through generous personal support of time, energy, and finance?

3. Specific Preparation for Action as a Trustee

- Is he/she apt to prepare himself/herself thoroughly for trustee meetings?
- Will he/she study and attempt to understand reports and background materials in advance of meetings?
- Can he/she be expected to ask probing and insightful questions at meetings focused on policy?
- Will he/she request and get information necessary for major decisions?

4. Ambassadorship

- Will he/she be an enthusiastic spokesperson for the organization who speaks often and intelligently of the institution to others?
- Will he/she often use contacts on behalf of the organization or suggest ways he/she can use contacts on behalf of specific programs?

5. Participation in Resource Development Programs

- Are his/her financial contributions meaningful in terms of his/her own resources?
- Can he/she be helpful in identifying prospects for all financial development programs?

- Will he/she help win financial support from others, through both direct and indirect personal participation?

6. Community Activity

- Can he/she be expected to serve usefully on one important committee?
- Will he/she suggest ideas, carry out duties, use his/her own abilities and influence constructively?

7. Attendance at Board Meetings and Committee Meetings

- Is he/she sufficiently interested and concerned about the organization to attend all scheduled meetings?

Governing Board Membership Criteria

Every nonprofit organization has statutory authority and responsibility for the management of an independent public trust on behalf of the people of the state in which the organization is incorporated. Therefore, each member of its governing board has both personal and joint responsibility, obligation, and accountability to determine and evaluate policies and procedures to ensure fulfillment of the chartered purposes of the organization. To these ends criteria for governing board membership shall include, but not be limited to, the following:

1. **Commitment.** Members must be deeply interested in and concerned for the fulfillment of the mission, goals, and objectives of the organization.

2. **Experience.** Members must have demonstrated civic, business, social, professional, and/or volunteer leadership experience important to the purposes of the organization.

3. **Builders.** Members must be dedicated to building a broad base of interest, respect, and financial support for the diverse goals, objectives, programs, services, events, and philanthropic requirements to serve the mission of the organization.

4. **Participation.** Members must consider and observe their role as a personal priority for *personal participation in all activities* of the organization.

5. **Support.** Members must be first investors in the philanthropic programs of the organization — general membership, gift club, current fund membership, special program and project support, and inclusion in bequests and estate plans for endowed fiscal stability and security to ensure the highest quality professional personnel and programs.

6. **Advocacy.** Pride in the organization's history calls for the broadest possible advocacy in all personal relationships — friends, business, community, and related activities for constant image building and broadest possible participation in programs and philanthropic investment support.

7. **Conflicts of Interest.** Members, their families, and business and professional associates must be free from the appearances of any form of conflict of interest in managing the affairs, policies, programs, procedures, and personnel of the organization.

The governing board, as a body and as individuals, serves as authenticators of the importance, integrity, independence, and confidence in and for the organization in terms of who they are as members, how they serve, and how they function for all local, regional, and national publics.

The member's personal and professional talent, skill, experience, wisdom, judgment, and generous philanthropic support set the pace *first* for both recognition and philanthropic support of the organization as it continues to serve future generations.

Composition of a Board of Trustees

The trustee statement on role and function is an expression of policy and aspiration for nonprofit board membership.

The degree to which the mission, goals, and objectives will be achieved depends to a significant extent on the composition and functions of the board of trustees. Realizing that individual members will not necessarily fulfill all qualifications, the ideal combination of factors serves as a model worth striving for.

A. Major Responsibilities.

1. *Orientation.* To become acquainted on site with the people, programs, and potential of the organization in fulfilling its leadership role among local and national competitors.

2. *Advocacy.* To seek opportunities for wide public advocacy of the organization and its potential; seek to influence friends and organizations for personal interest, concern, and philanthropic support of its values.

3. *Counsel.* To assist with wise and objective advice and judgment for the administration of the organization's resources — personnel, programs, plant, equipment, and finance. To assure that the organization adheres to its mission in all programs and outreach. To assist in setting broad, long-term objectives and goals to achieve them. To assess constantly assets and other resource needs.

4. *Finance.* To become the central leadership force in personal donations and then seeking gifts and grants to assure — even to insure — current budget adequacy as well as future stability and security. To initiate a comprehensive financial development program for current budget income, current capital asset, and endowment funds from estate and bequest sources.

B. Operations.

1. *Leadership.* To set criteria for board membership and continuous orientation about involuntary forces, issues, and trends affecting or likely to affect the organization.

2. *Preparation.* To assist by regular attendance at general and committee meetings for wise counsel as appropriate. To support the CEO in policy implementation by preparing as students of leadership through reading appropriate periodicals, publications, reports, and related materials.

3. *Channels.* Respect the chief executive officer of the organization as the formal channel and liaison between the board and internal constituents.

4. *Integrity.* Defend the organization, its management, staff, and students/patients/clients against attack by internal and external publics and organizations. Protect the organization's freedom as an independent force dependent upon private sector support.

C. Characteristics.

1. *Conviction.* Be convinced about the validity of the organization — its mission, its integrity, its values, its potential, and its requirements for financial asset-building.

2. *Commitment.* Be convinced of the organization's values and ethics as compatible with personal values for assurances of a certain future.

3. *Expertise.* Be of assistance as experience, talents, skills, and judgment have prepared each member for objective wisdom.

4. *Influence.* Serve as a bridge to the organization's constituencies for positive action on behalf of the organization.

5. *Philanthropy.* Possess a capacity to provide first and then to secure gifts and grants, which will inspire others to follow.

6. *Availability.* Be accessible for assumed board and committee responsibilities.

Trusteeship is not merely an honor. It is possessed of obligations and responsibilities of each person. That it reflects honor on an individual is secondary; the honor must not be misused nor abused in any manner in the name of the organization.

⚿ 2 ⮺
The Ministry of Philanthropy

I believe that every right implies a responsibility, every opportunity an obligation, every possession a duty.
— *John D. Rockefeller*

All who are served by our charitable organizations which receive donors' thoughtful gifts will be blessed in perpetuity because donors cared and donors shared.

Vision is the art of seeing things invisible.

Philanthropy? What is it?

The word philanthropy has a powerful and emotional meaning. The root is found in the Greek language. In Greek it is *philos anthropos*. It means "love of humankind." Philanthropy is expressed in different ways: gifts of leadership, gifts of influence, gifts of advocacy, gifts of time, gifts of wisdom, gifts of experience, and gifts of personal resources.

Every nonprofit organization stands as an active, human philanthropic asset meeting human needs. Every such vision begins with the founding of the organization. Each stands as a philanthropy expressing love, care, concern, and blessings for the humanitarian needs of the entire community, region, and nation.

Philanthropy is love of our fellow human being demonstrated. Philanthropy is never inactive. The widespread belief that the rich are overly philanthropic and the poor (those with an annual income of under $15,000) don't give enough is a myth.

The greatest philanthropist in the history of the world is the biblical widow. When she entered the temple, she deposited two mites, which was all the living she had (Luke 21:1-4). (See appendix D, page 225).

Every volunteer; every staff person; everyone who shares some of their current and estate resources; everyone who shares their talent, skills, wisdom or experience is an active philanthropist investing in the fulfillment of the ministry and mission of a philanthropy whether for religious, educational, cultural, healthcare, social or civic purposes.

Let's think, dream, talk, write, care, and share philanthropy philanthropically!

Philanthropy as a Ministry

Today our world society is more aware of our humanitarian interdependence than perhaps any time in history. Even with frequent and sustained local confrontations to the contrary, humanity's goal is human rights for all humankind. This goal is philanthropy applied, demonstrated, and provable. Human rights for all humankind is expressed through the positive love of one another regardless of origin, race, religion, culture, social, political, or economic conditions or differences. The goal is achieved through the ministry to each of God's children however God is expressed through individual and organizational caring and sharing without prejudice, arrogance, economic or social constraints. All that we are and all that we have we hold in trust for others as others have held in trust for us.

The essence of what I mean by philanthropy being a ministry is not that expressed alone by theologians, philosophers, psychologists or social scientists. Nor is what I mean by this title expressed by the financial gifts of money alone.

"Money is not wealth. Money cannot feed, shelter, or clothe man. By itself, money cannot give physical comfort to anyone. . . . Money is a promise for future goods or services," according to R.C. Sproul, Jr., in his book *Money Matters* (Tyndale House, 1985).

Perhaps the most profound demonstration of philanthropy administered by a body of people was recorded in a book by Dominique Lapierre, entitled *City of Joy* (Doubleday, 1985). This area in Calcutta, India, covers three football fields, yet houses some 70,000 people as a poverty-stricken industrial suburb. Even without adequate possessions for living, eating, clothing, without healthcare or drinking water; even with diseases of all kinds and known shortness of life expectancy, these people care for, share with, and look out for their neighbors constantly. They care for their fellow man whether eunuch, Catholic priest, medical doctor from Miami, Florida, or whomever. And they always express joy. They smile in spite of their stress or distress.

When the author was interviewed on television about his two years in the City of Joy, he said, "Coming to the studio up Fifth Avenue this morning, I noticed that not one of the well-dressed persons I passed smiled. In the City of Joy, everyone has a smile. What are we missing in our society?" Neither he nor the interviewer had an answer.

Perhaps the answer lies in the absence of care — caring enough to share, in the sharing to receive quiet, profound joy. To minister is to care. To care is to share. To share is to receive.

Webster defines philanthropy as "goodwill towards one's fellow men, especially as expressed through active efforts to promote human welfare; or, an act of deliberative generosity; or, an organization distributing funds for humanitarian purposes; an institution or agency supported by such contributions."

Too, Webster defines ministry as "the action of ministering the performance of any service or function for another."

In the world of promoting our philanthropies as facilities for greater and greater intrapersonal support of their humanitarian purposes, we must raise our consciousness beyond mere stewardship, mere charity, mere fund raising. As ministers, trustees, executives, staff, counsellors, and/or volunteers, we must first develop attitudes about the very essence of the spirit of philanthropy — a spiritual mandate — a personal mandate expressed through demonstrated stewardship, unconstrained charity, and unprecedented gift and grant productivity.

We have not begun to experience the full dimensions of available philanthropy because of our predisposition to numbers of donors rather than the breadth and depth of personal resources.

The ministry of philanthropy as a service or as an act of sharing time, talent, *and* treasure must not be a mere statement of intent. That ministry must be a demonstrated mandate for executing our trust responsibilities and obligations.

Inside every person is a philanthropist struggling to get out. One of the greatest limitations in our world of philanthropy is the lack of understanding that there is within all people a yearning to be a part of something larger than themselves. Recognizing that need and meeting it is the reward of our ministry for humankind.

We can take better aim in our ministry of philanthropy. Our target for productivity must be raised beyond the top of the hill of pitiful participation. We must raise the sights of both expectancy and personal/spiritual rewards. We must insure longer range goals through fiscal stability and security today.

We must think philanthropy, speak philanthropy, write, and publish philanthropy — not mundane fund raising. The world's humanitarian concerns will not be met through politics, economics, wars, social unrest, or star wars. Those concerns will be met through man's love for humankind demonstrated. Through the applied art of our philanthropic ministry, we can see solutions; without such ministry, only problems.

In our ministry, there is substance over style or expedience.

In our ministry, there are higher expectations for results because of better preparation, better listening, better thinking, better talking, better writing.

In our ministry there exists a better breadth and depth of attitudes about the productivity of time, talent, and treasure.

In our ministry, we must break new ground in perception, in application, in administration, and in productivity.

In our ministry, the management of our philanthropic motivations, inspirations, creativity, and application will help resolve world stress over human rights and help prevent other stress.

In our ministry, the philanthropic ideal is translatable, transferable, and transplantable by producing a spiritual change and increase in the depth of personal commitment, involvement, and fulfillment.

Man is an instrument of a higher order — a vessel found worthy to receive a divine influence. — Goethe

Every executive, volunteer, and staff person in our non-profit sector must elevate themselves in purpose above the necessary, but mundane, administrative responsibilities. These should be interpreted as the administration of our philanthropic ministry. Thus each and every constituent can be motivated to care about others and to share with others God's bountiful blessings that have been bestowed on us.

In 1986, an article, "It's Time to Start Doing Good," reported a real life story. Tom Anderson, an executive with the investment firm of Bear Stearns, cited his favorite book as the Bible. Yet, he was only a $2 collection plate donor at his church. He was challenged by reading in the Book of Malachi, "Will a man rob God? Yet ye have robbed me. But ye say, Wherein have we robbed thee? In tithes and offerings." In discussing this with a friend, the friend said to Tom, "Give God more money."

Tom wrote a check for $250 to World Vision. The next day, the very next day, an unproductive stock rose unexpectedly and covered the amount of the check. He gave away another $250. The same stock went up the next day. He sent $1,000 to philanthropy. The stock advanced again. He now says, "I've never seen anybody try to outgive God and come up short."

The whole philosophy of working at Bear Stearns is "We like to help human beings." The managing directors of Bear Stearns must give away a percentage of their salary and bonus. There a firm's employees are inspired to be donors — to be philanthropists. The firm is not the philanthropist. Herein is a lesson for treating and crediting all business firm matching gifts.

There exists a personal challenge in our role as ministers of philanthropy. That challenge lies in the proverbial three R's: recollection, reaffirmation, and renewal.

In the ministrations of our lives, our vocations, and avocations, let us *recall* what our associated organizations really mean as philanthropies — not just a church, a health-care institution, a college, or an association. Recall what the organization means to humankind as a deserving investment of the trust God gave each of us to hold for others — our resources, our nation, our concern for human dignity.

Now is the time for the *reaffirmation* of the limitless bounds of our organization as a philanthropy — not a material facility caring for people always and in all ways. Care for humanity, care for justice, care for abundance, care for demonstrations of love.

Let us renew our creative ingenuity toward philanthropic ideals of intellectual, spiritual, generous, loving functions of stewardship and charity. We must *renew* our expectations of unexpected results of our faith, our love, and our ministry. We must renew our commitment to our ideals expressed philan-thropically, not materially.

Our recollection results in our reaffirmation and renewal for new dimensions of our ministry for all of humankind.

Remember: A hand not extended in giving is in no position to receive.

Ensuring Our Values
through Philanthropy

Today when anyone talks about values at least two questions arise 1) whose values and 2) what values. To discuss values is like talking about quality and excellence. Our concepts of both remain but the evidence of both has faded in almost everything that we buy today. Individual, personal caring to ensure excellence has slipped from those who build, construct, create, and manufacture our acquisitions, thus eroding our concepts of high expectations and results of quality, excellence, and core values. Of greatest concern is the perception and respect of the priceless values of human life worldwide.

In spite of all of these concerns something else is happening to ensure our values of humanitarian services nationwide. We are witnessing in every nonprofit organization which is under progressive governance, serious, aggressive promotion of endowment funds calculated to ensure qualitative services of a stated mission called values inherent in that mission. These social, cultural, healthcare, educational, environmental, religious, humanitarian, and other programs and services of our nonprofit organizations have been recognized as human values which must be ensured. Basic, recurring programs and services may be sustained given present societal demands. But the startling demographics from our U.S. Census Bureau scares administrators in designs for strategic planning to prepare for the future now.

We see colleges, universities, hospitals, healthcare organizations, and homes for the elderly all seeking endowment funds from diverse personal resources. The purpose of income from endowment applies to personnel positions, programs, services, equipment, maintenance, and unrestricted purposes for uses not now foreseen.

The tremendous increase in the promotion of planned gift programs, plus advantageous federal tax savings, has encouraged bequest and estate plan gifts to reach a larger and larger percent of all philanthropic giving for all purposes. That percentage will double and triple and beyond as present planned-gift provisions mature.

Today every nonprofit organization must assess its value to society in terms of its productivity to meet diverse human needs. When is an organization worth 100 million, 200 or 500 million, one billion, now with Harvard conducting a two billion, 100 million endowment program? Cornell University concluded its one and a quarter billion capital fund program on December 31, 1995. They did not make their goal. They exceeded by one quarter billion. Ninety percent of that result came from three and a half percent of their constituents.

Such achievements of core values demand great mental attitude changes from those just seeking to get by with a balanced annual budget. Those trustees and administrators devoted only to survival, in fact, are presiding over the eventual demise of their organization. These governors of a statutory public trust are merely custodians of the status quo, not builders of a positive destiny. This is why so many symphony, ballet, and other cultural organizations, colleges, and hospitals are on the brink of closure or merger. We have lost some 500 small, independent colleges since 1970 and they are not missed. Why are they not here? They were non-managed by their governing board. They were sustained but not insured to thrive. And the corpus of their fiscal growth, security, and sustentation had to be substantial to meet the *involuntary* growth of our national economy and demographics.

Your constituents, your prospects need to know your assessment of the value of your organization to society, not just today, but its worth 10 years from now. That value assessment must be realistic in terms of costs of excellence and qualities in all features and functions. And you must not apologize for the costs of quality in your history, your mission, your present status and probable costs, not of survival, but thriving. Once determined, then you must "sell" that value to your constituents, not ask them if your organization is worth it.

Many colleges, universities, and hospitals are seeking philanthropic funds of high eight, nine, and 10 figures to *insure* their value and values as an *indispensable* entity ever ready to meet humanitarian needs.

Those endowments must be broken down into "sales" units for people to provide as their personal investments. Those units must be set as a corpus need to produce an income of value even 20 years from now.

Such items listed should begin with taking out of the budget all possible items to be sustained by endowment income. Such commitments now for "preferred use" endowed functions frees operating funds for features not budgeted and for increased costs of operation bound to come. The presentation of these investment gift opportunities is a marketing procedure. Your constituents know that these features exist on a daily basis of application. They do not know that they can be purchased and insured for use in perpetuity. Thus they, in fact, are buying a value important to them which they wish to secure in fulfillment of the mission of the organization which they hold to have lasting value.

One of the most popular administrative decisions today is to initiate a vision of the future and a strategic plan. Countless well-meaning consultants are retained to assess what is, then project its future, and conclude its indispensability. Almost never is a function recommended for discontinuance, regardless of its low value. Nearly every strategic plan, when completed, is termed immortal. No one dares contest it! Yet, when completed, it never assesses the value of what is or what is to come. Never is there a cost projection of the value of implementation and continuation. Yet, quality costs, excellence costs, values cost.

If values eventually come out of a strategic plan for short-term or long-term fulfillment, then a "feasibility study" is initiated to determine if the organization is worth projected costs for proposed values. Yet, respondents were not party to the strategic plan effort nor its consequences. How do they know to answer honestly? It is the obligation of the organization to "sell" their values, elevating perceptions from the VW Bug to the majestic Mercedes. People — individuals, couples, families — await the opportunity to *"buy" valuable philanthropic investments.* But if they are never offered, they are never purchased (by cash, investment resources, real estate, life insurance no longer needed, or various planned gift instruments).

We insure our lives, our homes, our valuables but not our values. Our nonprofit organizations are indispensable values to our society — to every living human being. Caring for ourselves by ourselves was a revelation beyond understanding by a Frenchman, Alexis de Tocqueville, in 1830. He was here three years to study prisons. But he also observed what to him was a social phenomenon. He found it curious when people in a community saw a need and set up a plan among themselves to meet that need even from their own funds. To him this was a revelation. They did it by themselves for themselves. He saw us as a strange people but a happy nation. He wrote about us in his book *Democracy in Action.*

Our ancestors could not count upon public funds, which I call "involuntary philanthropy." And today we cannot count upon such funds however we have legislated for them. Even tax exemption privileges stress preference for private philanthropy. The results are in our hands. Our values are our concern, our responsibility, our opportunity — voluntary philanthropy.

We are responsible for ensuring our values if organizations will just tell us the costs of those values to ensure them in perpetuity and how to preserve them.

Raising Millions Instead of Thousands

Today, we are mere spectators of incredible humanitarian, spiritual, social, economic, and political changes never before dreamed of without the consequences of wars. Perhaps it can be said that not since besieged people of Europe sought refuge in an unknown country now called the United States have people taken up their hands and hearts instead of weapons to initiate a voluntary ministry of humankind's divine rights in seeking freedom from involuntary oppression. (See appendix E, page 227.)

Yes, millions and millions of persons have raised their sights of life and living, seeking respect, unrestrained opportunity, greater abundance of necessities, and fiscal stability and security.

The Bible deals with money and resources in 16 of the 38 parables and one verse in six discusses the correct way to handle possessions.

In the world of promoting our philanthropies — churches, organizations, services — as vehicles for greater and greater intrapersonal support of their humanitarian purposes, we must raise our consciousness beyond mere stewardship, mere charity, or mere fund raising.

We have not begun to experience the full dimensions of available philanthropy because of our predisposition to counting numbers of donors rather than the breadth and depth of personal resources (assets) present as well as personal interests and concerns. Our targets for financial productivity must be raised beyond the top of the hill of pitiful participation. We must insure longer range goals for fiscal stability and security.

Since my entrance in this field in 1948, every year individuals have counted for 85 percent to 90 percent of all funds and resources given. In the last 15 years the numbers of individuals with annual incomes of one million dollars or more have grown from 300,000 to 720,000. It has been estimated recently that this number will increase by 100,000 each year. Those with annual incomes of $10 million or more have been reported at over 81,000 persons.

In 1983, I began tabulating all gifts of $1,000,000 or more which I saw announced in any publication. There were 243, of which 122 were individuals or families. In 1995, I saw 1,110 such gifts announced, of which 528 were individuals or families. Because most associations of philanthropies do not encourage members to report such gifts for national publication there are undoubtedly four or five times this number of seven-, eight-, and nine-figure gifts.

The point is that donors with such resources look for confidence in the composition of governing boards, policies for experienced investment counsellors, sound long-term planning goals and objectives, pride and gratitude for services rendered, and in administrative and programmatic leadership.

Claude Rosenberg, Jr., in his book *Wealthy and Wise: How You and America Can Get the Most Out of Your Giving* (Little, Brown, 1994) proves that philanthropy *is missing out on at least $100 billion a year* from living individuals and families. To achieve this, nonprofits must redefine and reinvest the way donor/investors are identified, researched, and shown diverse investment gift options. That book is *an absolute must* for all nonprofit executives, trustees, and staff members. Herein lies the goal of seeking numbers of dollars from five percent of constituents, not high-cost production of numbers of donors/investors.

Does your organization have a short-term and long-term design for its destiny together with current fund, special program and project, as well as endowment costs? If not, destiny has a design awaiting.

Does your organization recognize every donor as an investor (not a supporter) in the assurance of quality mission achievements?

Does your organization promote diverse named investment gift opportunities for endowment by gift commitments now and/or by bequest or estate plan instruments?

Does your organization have sound investment policies and use experienced investment counsellors for maximum income return and security?

Does your organization need annual, weekly, monthly contributions endowed forever? Do you say so?

Does your organization just *beg* for mendicancy, *appeal* for mediocrity, and pass tin cans for quarters? Herein lies no gratitude, no pride, no future.

In the ministry of our organizations and our lives, our vocations, our avocations, our services, let us recall what our ministries mean as a philanthropy — not just another nonprofit organization.

Let us raise our attitudes to that of *investing* in our philanthropies.

Let us design our destiny without apology in assessing financial goals for financial worth.

Let us think millions, not thousands.

Let us prepare for and expect investments of greater commitments than ever before because we have designed our destiny, determined the costs of that destiny, educated our constitutents about how to become greater philanthropists, and enlisted only those volunteers who themselves are creative spokespeople for greater philanthropy.

Let us apply our creative energies and expectations toward philanthropic ideals of intellectual, spiritual, generous, loving functions of stewardship and charity to philanthropy.

We must recognize that millions in diverse resources are there and in greater abundance than ever, but they must be requested for and earned by deserving organizations as gifts of *confidence, pride, and gratitude.*

∞ *3* ∞

The Motivation of
Giving: The Philosophy
of Philanthropy

*The root of excellence is the freedom to dream the
unthinkable and to finance the impossible.*

A hand not extended in giving is in no position to receive.

To examine the philosophy of philanthropy is to examine the
mysteries of a universal social phenomenon that go to the
very heart of humanity's spiritual values: that which defines
who we are, what we hope for, what we cherish; or simply,
why we do what we do.

    I understand that Aristotle was a philosopher, although
he would not have called himself that; he was just a man who
wanted to understand. He started his work, his journey toward
understanding, right where he was, by observing the things
around him, the way the world functioned. From the knowledge he gained first through his observations, Aristotle formulated his physics. We know now, however, many of his
deductions about the physical world, while advanced for his
day, were subsequently proven to be wrong.

But Aristotle's need to understand extended beyond the physical world around him into the hearts of people with whom he lived and worked. So, in like manner to his physical observations, he studied people and asked why they did what they did. Out of the wisdom he gained from these observations, he formulated his ethics, his first principles of human conduct. His ethics still stand today. Their validity is rooted in the mysteries I referred to earlier.

Aristotle could make his observations of human conduct because, being human, he first observed himself. He could observe what went on inside himself, his own feelings and then ponder the "why" — the substance — of those feelings. As it turns out, he was much more correct about his perceptions of people's motivations than about physics.

Learned observers explaining why Aristotle was right more so in one area and wrong in another have distinguished between intrinsic and extrinsic motivation or casualty. That persistent phenomenon without a science is intrinsic motivation, the analysis of why people do what they do, in other words, actions which defy precise mechanistic motivation. Extrinsic motivation, really cause and effect, has little to do with intrinsic actions and that motivation can be measured precisely.

What I have to say next about intrinsic motivation will make no sense to the purely technical fund raiser, the computer devotee, the progenitor of glossy publications or those devoted to mathematic analyses of mechanical results. Here I am concerned that those devoted exclusively to "how to" workshops, seminars, institutes, and artificial curricula for certification will not even recognize, let alone understand, that intrinsic motivation exists. Look how long it has taken this very subject — exploring the philosophy of philanthropy — to appear on a public platform. If we are to graduate from the limiting statistics of fund raising in reverence of extrinsic evidence up to the limitless consequences of philanthropy, we must explore the intrinsic evidences of human actions and loose our constituents for the impact upon humanity within their capabilities.

Like Aristotle, if we observe ourselves first as philanthropists, if we observe why we gave, and why we have not done so *a priori* before we ask others, we could better understand the intrinsic values that motivate or do not motivate those whom we seek to share their resources eagerly, generously, philanthropically. Unfortunately, those who seek philanthropy often participate the least when they are asked.

The realist in me says that we must begin by observing real things just as Aristotle started by observing the people and the things around him. Only then can we come to a philosophy of philanthropy as Aristotle came to his metaphysics. Just as the Greeks looked at the stars and began to wonder why they appeared to be moving, we must look at what moves us to do what we do, why we do it, and why we do not do other things. As we observe nature, physics, and even metaphysics, we observe change, motion, myths, and perceptions. We found out long after the Greeks perceived that the stars moved, that they do not move. We do. Maybe, just maybe, there is not a real philosophy of philanthropy, but isn't it time that we wonder why not, why not now, why not here? Let us observe some intrinsic motivations.

Why is it that a secondary school trustee developed the compelling urge to give $250,000 long before his resource development committee was ready to announce a formal asset-building program. He convinced three other persons to join him in providing the school's first one-million-dollar gift to its first endowment fund. And each did so anonymously.

Why does an alumna of a women's college provide the school an annual gift in the amount of the current tuition charge even though her tuition in the 1930s was a fraction of today's costs?

Why did an alumna of the class of 1973 provide her college a copy of her will in 1975 thereby advising that she committed $750,000 for the endowment of a professorship?

None of these commitments were requested.

By what criteria, by what perceptions, by what system of values or ethics were these voluntary commitments made? Psychologists would be quick to deduce motivations of self-gratification, fear, reward mechanisms, guilt, anxiety, and many other negative aspects as reasons. But are negative reasons alone valid?

Did those of you think about these things when you decided to provide a gift — an act of selflessness we honor?

Did those of you who seek philanthropic gift commitments prepare yourself in attitude or conscience that you were providing others the opportunity for unselfish personal fulfillment?

Did those of you think about these things when you requested your prospects to share their resources for others not themselves?

We do not make anyone give; the philosophic phenomenon is the giving!

Why did a substantial business executive, alumnus, and parent persuade a university president to consider his wife as the prospect for a large philanthropic commitment? He had already given $500,000. He told the president that he wanted his wife personally to experience the great joy he had experienced when he did what he did. Also, he added, she would undoubtedly survive him and be able to give a great deal more than he could.

Why did a trustee and alumna bring her daughter and son into providing nearly a two-million-dollar gift to her college?

Why do many families encourage living heirs to experience the joy of giving?

That joy is contagious. Sharing frees one from the artificial bonds of withholding. As we seek the wisdom in what we do, all other things will be added unto us.

True philanthropy cannot be the result of manipulation no matter how adept the manipulator. As human beings being pressed quickly into an increasingly mechanistic society, we seldom take time to reason why. Why does the simple calculator work? We may not know; but someone does. Why does the computer work ever more simply? We may not know; but someone does. Why do we give of our resources voluntarily without pressure of the law of recrimination? We just simply do not know. Is it time that we examine ourselves positively so that we make it possible to help others share in the consummate joy of the spiritual essence of philanthropy?

Can you imagine the supreme joy experienced by a donor of $18 million when he heard a college president say that he could not build a great college because of the press of urgent housekeeping maintenance needs? The donor inquired about those pressing needs, their amount, and then said, "I'll provide that amount to meet those needs; now build your great college."

What manner of deep, personal gratification did these persons experience? Could it be the same unselfish love of the gift of the library of John Harvard? Could it be the same spirit of providing for others which resulted in the creation of seminaries, schools, colleges, hospitals, and community organizations? This spirit is an innate human characteristic yearning for the occasion, yearning for the opportunity to share gratitude if the people but knew where, through whom, and how. How can we avoid looking into the intrinsic motivations of ourselves and others as we seek financial stability and security for our institutions?

This process of voluntary sharing we call philanthropy. John D. Rockefeller III in his book *The Second American Revolution* (Harper & Row, 1973) said that the word philanthropy is too sophisticated for the average American because it relates to the great, often heralded philanthropists like his father, Andrew Carnegie, and others. He suggested referring to the private sector as the independent sector, thus even further depersonalizing the sublime act of sharing personal resources. Could it be that even he forgot that the widow referred to in the Bible was a true philanthropist who gave all of the little she had while rich men cast little of their riches into the treasury?

Let us be proud of philanthropy — the word, the spirit, the act, the result. Let us understand that philanthropy is a sublime demonstration of man's caring for his fellow man. Let us reach and teach others that sharing our resources, be they small or large, is a demonstration of true caring. Let us disown proclamations that generous giving is the result of greed, guilt, fear, ego, recognition.

We see the results of philanthropy — gifts of time, gifts of leadership, gifts of wisdom, gifts of judgment, gifts of dreaming the impossible — in the faculty and staff of our diverse, unselfish, serving institutions. Their service amid meager budgets, maintenance too long deferred, salaries we would not accept, endowments far from insuring fiscal stability, qualifies them for generosity earned and deserved. Those who staff and serve amid these limitations but serve on are true philanthropists, too. They often go unrecognized. But they serve. They do not represent greed, guilt, fear, ego or request recognition. But they give. We are surrounded by philanthropists within our institutions!

What then is the philosophy of philanthropy?

What is the measure of our satisfaction in giving when we are not required to do so? Can we measure satisfaction without perceiving the ingredients which cause the result?

Why is it that one husband and wife team gave a college a new residence hall without expecting honor or name recognition? The need existed. The donors created the opportunity. When done, they asked the college, "What else do you need?" They were told of the burden of a persistent accumulated debt of nearly $700,000. The mandatory interest payments up front impeded quality additions to the academic program and student assistance. They offered to eliminate the debt in one year if the college could increase annual fund support from under $200,000 to $350,000 by the next June 30. Next June the college reported gifts totalling $480,000 with one gift of $10,000. All other gifts were less. $480,000 + $700,000 plus interest no longer due over an anticipated long term has had a gigantic impact on that college. The donors sought no honor. There was no guilt complex. There was no fear of lack of funds for the future.

Why did they do this?

I believe that it was because they cared. They sought to reward the college for earned and deserved philanthropy. They believed in the mission of the college. They believed that the college administration deserved relief from the anxiety of involuntary budget contraints affecting the very integrity of the institution, present and future students, quality education.

I believe that in our race for massive fund raising — a term I seek to avoid as synonymous with mendicancy, begging, mechanical stimulation — we are seeking quarters for parking meters. Let us recognize that we are engaged in philanthropy.

Let us begin to study the motivations of philanthropy — the innate desires of people to share, to share generously.

Let us set aside the seeming preoccupation of psychologists who document humanity's negative motivations and now begin to study anew the positive aspects awaiting — concerned, objective, revelation.

I believe that there are at least six basic positive motivations for true, generous philanthropy. These are: the desire to express faith; to express love for one's fellow man; to perpetuate the American dream; to help secure or assure; to help build; and to invest. Please permit me to qualify these as a basis for other persons to ponder, to study, to analyze, to research for the future. At the same time, permit me to offer one basic criterion for that person or those persons who will undertake to study the positive aspects of the motivations of philanthropy. Future researchers must be free from the contagion of philanthropic impotence. To authenticate their analyses, their research, their prognostications, they must have experienced personally the exhilaration of sacrificial giving of their hard-earned personal resources. Without this *a priori* academic, social, and spiritual experience, their work must be considered antiseptic.

Six Motivations for Philanthropy

First, the desire to express faith means to me humanity's innate desire to offer a vote of confidence and an expression of approval in the mission, the goals, the services, the leadership of the organization. This vote of support demonstrated is the external manifestation of the proclamation: I believe in you, what you stand for, what you are doing — as president, as a trustee, as a volunteer, as a staff member, as an organization. If you were not accomplishing these things, I would like to do so. The least I can do is to help you do so.

Second, the desire to express one's love for his fellow man. To me this desire is the active demonstration of the reflection of

God through one person or family for others. This reflective action is perhaps intentional, but perhaps unintentional, as the result of early teaching at home and in houses of worship. How else is man to reflect God except through works He would do? Who is to say that such works demonstrated are not His will externalized? Think of those now gone who built for us today.

Third, the desire to perpetuate the American dream is not a salute to chauvanism (false pride) nor to jingoism (American right or wrong). Here I am talking about real love of country; real patriotism; gratitude for our freedom of choice, freedom to earn; freedom to prevent the necessity for government to do what we can do faster, at less cost and for greater human benefit. I believe in the "No Deposit; No Return" statement: unless we put into the American privilege of freedom of choice, we can expect no return; indeed, we have no right of return.

Fourth, the desire to help, to assure. Here generous, unselfish donors seek to guarantee opportunity for others; guarantee services; guarantee personal, career, social, spiritual, cultural, financial growth. Too few of our deserving organizations achieve fiscally secure and stable guarantees. We are not creating enough future Harvards, Yales, Princetons, Stanfords!

Fifth, the desire to help build. Here is the zeal for entrepreneurship at its best. We in America have capitalized on our zeal to create, to build — programs, courses, committees, and, yes, buildings. But we build without providing basic insurance of utility of that which is built. We start but we do not insure that which we have built. But we build so that we can see. We must build and insure by endowing that which we build.

Sixth, the desire to invest. Investors are not builders of external, visible symbols. Investors are guarantors; they want to perpetuate ideas, concepts, ideals, visions, proof of utility, that which is proven good, and to ensure credibility and confidence.

And there may be more innate human desires in the demonstration of philanthropy — the demonstration of man's love for man.

As we explore the philosophy of philanthropy today, what are your criteria, what are your motivations, what are the dimensions of your philanthropic potential as you try to persuade others to do what you have not done proportionate to your capability? And, for those who have begun to experience the rewards of sharing, perhaps you have but tested the waters of love expressed awaiting your decision.

The demonstrations of philanthropy are neither insular nor antiseptic; indeed, they are contagious. We cannot revel in what we have done. We haven't even started to give what we can to share generously of that which we have.

Consider if you will your priorities — your philanthropic priorities. Explore your reasons, your prejudices, your objectives, your ethics, your values as you share your resources voluntarily. Are you really generous? Or is your generous impulse restrained by fear of lack rather than expectancy of adequacy? If you as askers do not give generously, could it be that that fact transmits itself unknowingly when you ask others to share?

If you give in fear, is this not anti-philanthropy, not quite confident of God's love to provide as He asks you to do?

Exploring philanthropy is exploring ourselves. There is so much to learn, so much to understand, so much to prove. The occasion is our beginning today.

Remember: A hand not extended in giving is in no position to receive,

And: Money/resources are the roots of all excellence.

Why People Give; Why They Don't

Inspiring Others to Give

Creating the desire to give, then to give generously, then to give recurringly, then to give ultimately by bequest is the continuing challenge of staff personnel, officers, governing board members, and volunteers alike. Those who find the secret to the challenge, succeed; those who don't, move on.

How can those who have never experienced the inner joy of generous giving themselves ever hope to inspire others, to find the secret of the challenge of wanting to give more than anything else in life? This question applies to each and every staff member of every nonprofit organization, to each and every staff officer, to each and every governing board member. The conviction that resonates from a deep personal commitment speaks more loudly than any case statement, any film, any brochure, any letter. And such resonance can only be transmitted in a personal meeting to discuss the philosophy, the spirit, the psychology of philanthropy. The key word here is philanthropy. Philanthropy, not fund raising. Not mendicancy. Not begging. Not participatory percentages, or averages, or gift-range tables. Philanthropy! ". . . love of humankind."

No one is required to give of their resources to anyone for anything ever!

Only to the extent that governing board members, volunteers, officers, and staff personnel plan ways to motivate, to persuade, to encourage unselfish investment in voluntary human endeavors — just to that extent will they be successful and successful beyond their expectations. (See appendix C, page 223.)

Planning Financial Support Programs

The planning of financial support programs requires several specific functions if substantial support is needed, earned, and deserved.

The organization. First, the organization must know where it's going. It must design its destiny in both qualitative and quantitative terms and cost them out honestly and totally. If they don't, destiny has a design for them!

Future investors. Second, it must position itself in several dimensions to earn the confidence it seeks from future investors. This positioning includes: (1) building a governing board composed of powerful members of influence or affluence or both; (2) implementing a marketing strategy to promote the organization's integrity, its values, its services, its potential; (3) communicating its values and vision in every media form to that 10 percent of its constituents who hold in their hands and hearts the power to affect the destiny of the organization; (4) studying its constituency resource principals to ascertain their interests, concerns, ideals, and personal nuances; (5) ascertaining the personal needs of those few constituents so as to set a strategy for an eventual investment commitment; and (6) creating an asset-builder/building psychology among all other constituents. This is quite an order! So be it. That is what philanthropy is all about. All the rest is mere fund raising — a set of mechanics.

The staff. Third, there must be a staff that is capable of managing the plan for a certain destiny, the positioning functions and the implemental features of any program whether for annual support of operations, for special projects, for endowment or all of these simultaneously under a comprehensive resource development plan.

Prospect cultivation plan. Fourth, there must be a prospect cultivation plan to establish awareness of the organization's design for its destiny, to create interest of the prospects in the organization, to induce involvement in diverse ways, to inculcate concern that the organization flourish, and to gain a commitment to its financial stability and security.

Psychology of giving. Fifth, there must be an understanding on the part of all staff and volunteers about the psychology of philanthropic giving. Cultivating and soliciting key financial support prospects is a delicate art in human relations. Only those individuals who possess the talent, spirit, and experience for these delicate negotiations should be trained and trusted for large gift solicitation — investments to insure the future.

These factors are important if any organization seeks greater and greater private sector support from individuals, families, businesses, foundations or other organizations.

What about the Donor?

The spirit. All donors are people, whether business or foundation executives, alumni, patients or friends. They have feelings. They also have prejudices. They have ideals. They have fears. But even more, they have a spirit. The act of philanthropy is a spiritual act — an act of love expressed for one's fellow man. The voluntary motivation of giving or granting is also an intangible act. Pieces of paper may be exchanged in the process, but the sharing and the receiving is intangible in concept and in precept. Persons who share the resources they own or control buy pride in identification, satisfaction in accomplishment, or promise for the future.

Case history. The president of a small college took a new trustee on a driving tour of the campus. The president pointed out where a new science building could be built among some 80 houses and three former churches constituting the college campus. Well along in the tour, the trustee asked if the president had ever thought about an entirely new campus. The president parked the car to prevent an accident! He told the trustee of the founder's dream, which he shared, to build the college on an estate at the end of Main Street. The trustee asked to see the estate. It was still there — in ruin. The next stop was the real estate agent. The trustree bought the 1,000 acres and said: "Now build your dream college." And they did.

Why do people give? Why don't they?

Why? We don't take time to study the "why" of our own gift response. Why do we give and give generously? Why don't we give? Regardless of the size of our giving are we proud of our "widow's mite" philanthropically? What kind of an example are we? Who is reaching us to induce a true philanthropic investment, pride in joining, confidence in management, competence of leadership, evidence of a certain future, evidence of integrity in services? Belief in the very ideal and plan we are promoting begins with our own personal philanthropic commitment.

But this statement is supposed to be about others, not us. They are us. As we think of ourselves, only then can we plan for the motivation of others. What is our dream? Where is our dream? In whom are we investing? Are we providing for others as others have provided for us? Are we investing in the organization in which we expect others to invest to the fullest extent of their capacity? Are we insuring the values of the organization for future generations?

Positioning for Investments

The art of positioning an organization for generous response requires openness in explaining multiple investment opportunities; investing in current operational support; investing in special projects; and investing in endowment. It's appropriate to address all constituents at the beginning of the fiscal year reporting on the multiple financial needs to sustain services and the multiple resources individuals have to invest in gift opportunities from income, plus some portion of current assets, plus estate assets. But first, it's important to consider how the prospective donor would answer the following questions.

Checklist of questions to consider

Voluntary giving must be earned or deserved as a result of good management of resources in fulfilling the organization's mission. Then, to the extent that the presentation is sound, honest, reasonable, and persuasive, the potential donor may become a donor in fact. What is the potential donor's position? What are the thought processes of the prospect to ascertain whether or not to participate, at what level, when, and how? The following points suggest questions staff and volunteers must consider, transplanting themselves mentally to the prospect's position when asked to invest in the requesting organization:

- ✔ Was the request for the solicitation interview thoughtful, well stated, honest?
- ✔ Were the volunteer/staff solicitors well prepared, as interested about me/us? Did they give evidence that they really knew me/us sufficiently?
- ✔ Did they get to the point in good time?
- ✔ Did they really know the organization, the plan, the program?
- ✔ Was the specific request well stated for a range of giving or merely a yes-or-no figure? Was it reasonable for me/us given knowledge of my/our background?
- ✔ Was the presentation persuasive or matter-of-fact? Were solicitors enthusiastic? Concerned for the urgency of success?
- ✔ Is the organization really doing the job the solicitors stated? More so? Or less so? Was their evidence convincing?

✔ Am I/we satisfied with and/or grateful for the organization's services?

✔ Do I/we really know the organization's leadership, management, staff, volunteers?

✔ Is the organization really well-managed?

✔ Is the plan for the future reasonable, impressive, persuasive?

✔ Will my/our investment make a difference?

✔ Should I/we provide a modest gift as a test of the organization's efficiency and see how the program progresses or should I/we provide a real gift of confidence in the organization — its plan, leadership, volunteers?

✔ How does this request fit into my/our priorities — family security, current financial and imminent obligations, career investments, other philanthropies, social responsibilities — or none of these?

✔ Is this my/our best investment for my/our interests, concerns, ideals? Is this where we should put back/ provide for others as others have provided for us?

✔ Who else is supporting the organization? What is their record? What is the record of the governing board participation?

✔ Did the presenters say what they were giving?

✔ Are those gift clubs really important for current fund giving? Are all those benefits really necessary? How much do they cost? Do I/we want to get that involved? Or should I/we be anonymous?

✔ Why didn't the presenters mention endowing my/our gift since they talked about a long-range plan?

✔ Why should I/we decide now?

✔ Did the presenters mention monthly payments (they would be much easier to reach the figures they mentioned)?

✔ Is now the time for me/us to provide a really significant gift?

✔ What is the best way to do it? Maybe we should talk to their planned gift officer as they mentioned?

✔ Do I/we want our gift to be unrestricted, designated for budget items or something else?

✔ Small gifts really don't add up — but how much should I/we give, the largest sum the presenters mentioned, the smaller or the one they mentioned first?

And so it goes. All of these questions and more can occur quickly or can require months before a final decision. The point is that each potential donor is far from an easy touch. Each person weighs his or her participation in terms important to him or her first, then of importance to the organization. The better the solicitors are trained for a low-key, sophisticated, persuasive presentation, the quicker will be the prospect's decision. Also, the selection of solicitors who are comfortable with the solicitation — intangible sales — process, the more productive the interview and the earlier a decision can be expected.

Reasons for Giving

The art of solicitation involves both a philosophical and a psychological dimension based on prospect research and resulting in a presentation strategy. Not every solicitation should be identical if success is intended. People are different. Personal situations are different. The solicitation environments are different. But when the question is asked, people revert to basic, personal criteria for an ultimate decision. Some of these, which appear in various academic and promotional contexts, are:

- Demonstrated spiritual love for humankind gained from spiritual teachings.
- Philanthropic concern for humankind through gifts of time or resources or both.
- Experiences gained from family teachings of sharing possessions or resources with others.
- Personal gratitude for life or services rendered.
- Perpetuation of personal ideals, values, and goals.
- Personal pride in achievement and caring for others.
- Joining in success to assure organizational goals.
- Fear — prevention of want, assurance of services.

- Tax considerations. Many solicitors would add tax considerations as a crucial factor in philanthropic gift decision-making. For some potential donors, tax considerations are major considerations. But even for them, the decision to give or not to give to any particular organization is based on non-tax considerations first, given the options to give to other philanthropies.

Reasons for Not Giving

The reasons people *don't* give are crucial factors for all governing board members, officers, staff, and volunteers to study before launching any philanthropic financial support program. Some of these reasons are:

- Absence of a reasonable plan for future stability and security (a reflection on management and administration).
- Absence of powerful authenticators for the organization represented by governing board members and volunteers.
- Concern for human, facility, and service management.
- Concern for investment policies represented by inadequate return.
- Inadequate communications about the dynamics and finances of the organization.
- Inadequate prospect research to ascertain those who hold in their hands and hearts the power to affect the destiny of the organization.
- Unfortunate combination of persons as the solicitation team.
- Premature determination of potential donor's readiness to give now and to provide a substantial commitment.
- Failure to ask for a gift size commensurate with the scope of the case for support.
- Failure to recommend that the donor use multiple resources for the gift request.
- Failure to include the spouse in cultivation and presentation meetings.

- Mechanical, impersonal solicitations.
- Failure to suggest a specific gift objective within the program goals and case statement.
- Failure in debriefing specifics following cultivation and solicitation visits.
- Failure in sensitive follow-up.

The donor's needs prevail. Unfortunate experiences of volunteers and professionals alike could add to this list. It's even more unfortunate that volunteers, officers, governing board members, and even staff members press for fast prospect gift decisions, forsaking the necessity for careful strategy before solicitation. There is a strong supposition that the organization's needs dominate all reason and rationality — even that of the potential donor, never considering adequately the perceived needs of the prospect. In the final analysis, the donor's needs prevail. And to the extent they do prevail, just to that extent will the organization's needs be met. Philanthropic giving is a two-way street. When two needs meet, investments result.

Prevailing Assumptions of Human Behavior

Let's examine some factors of human behavior experienced, studied, and assumed to be in the hearts and minds of potential donors.

Assume that people want to belong. They want to belong to a success, to be part of a success.

Each person must be convinced of his or her importance in resolving a need in terms of evaluation of his or her part.

People evaluate the logic of the program and plan presented.

People assess their confidence in both administrators and managers.

People are complimented by being asked to give at a level and at a time that are in line with their estimate of their capacity and the impact of their leadership position.

People who are the potential donors are the only ones to decide what their gift will be and how they will provide it and when.

People are turned off by legal pledges, preferring "statements of intent" or "commitments of confidence" as sufficient evidence of their intended transfer of cash or other resources.

People who aren't asked to give according to their own estimate of their capacity know at once that:

- The solicitor isn't convinced of the importance of the plan, program or projects.
- The solicitor has not given himself/herself.
- Homework hasn't been done as to the prospect's importance and potential, or
- A carefully studied financial support plan doesn't exist.

People who are prospects for above-average gift support merit a personal call by at least one person, preferably two but never three, and may be turned off when solicited by letter or phone.

People subconsciously determine their gift participation relative to the total goal sought.

People act relative to goals and to deadlines.

People resent begging, pressure, and deficits.

People respond to competence and confidence in solicitors with whom they come in contact.

The solicitor must be sensitive to the prospect's anguish to make the right decision, know the virtues and goals of the organization, and be persuasive but never demanding. There is a chasm of difference between the impulsive donor; the habitual donor of small amounts; the thoughtful, careful donor who responds to sophisticated tender loving care but who does his or her own checking as to the validity of the organization.

The meeting of organizational needs with prospective donors' needs for personal fulfillment becomes a mutuality of concerns and respect. Thoughtful giving begins with thoughtful asking, always seeking an understanding as to why people give and why they don't.

Motivation for Philanthropic Productivity

Philanthropy in our country stands as an invaluable, indispensable tradition of caring for our neighbors and our communities. That motivation of caring causes voluntary sharing of our time, talent, and treasure to ensure comfort, hope, and freedom from fear. The act of philanthropy constitutes an applied ministry of humanitarian needs in serving others as others have provided for us. Such giving of ourselves is entirely voluntary. No one is ever required to give. Such expressions of love are investments in those about whom we care and for whom we share of ourselves and our God-given resources we hold in trust for others. The United States stands as the world model for private sector action now being copied aggressively worldwide.

Ever since records have been kept on who gives what to whom, individual, family, and estate gifts have constituted 85 percent to 90 percent of all gifts recorded year after year — not business firms, not general foundations.

The federal and state regulations to provide a tax deduction to gift and grant donors have served as stimuli for increased voluntary philanthropy. Those stimuli eliminated the necessity for governments to step in and take over fiscal controls of organizations. Had they done so, today's tax burden would be even further beyond comprehension.

To analyze the features and factors of motivation for generous philanthropy, one must begin with theological, sociological, psychological, and philosophical issues and factors. Such factors are deeply personal. Too, those factors may be different for each person. Therefore, any prospect research to ascertain what feature will motivate generous commitments from any one prospect becomes very intangible and variable. To understand why people who have the appearance of unusual resource capacity — individuals, families, business executives, and foundation executives — do not give or do give generously becomes complex. Yet, they must be studied to determine their motivation and the recipients' strategies as human resource analysts.

Perhaps those affiliated with healthcare institutions and organizations are confronted by the most dramatic of all human motivational concerns. The innate desire to live as long as possible in the healthiest of all possible conditions possesses every living person. Efforts to ensure, then insure, human physical and mental perfection becomes causitive motivation to do whatever is necessary.

Outside rests the probability that present and continual and increasingly generous philanthropy can provide the means for solving every problem. While money and resources may be the roots of all excellence, those roots must be combined with experienced and dedicated personnel, education, research, and the art and science of intellectual ingenuity.

These features described and certified as present, awaiting only the revelation of time to prove what is suspected, become the "sales force" of motivating confidence to invest in the process. The investment, therefore, intends to accelerate the process of resolution.

Seldom, very, very seldom, are potential investors of truly large amounts ever given the opportunity to "make a difference" by providing an investment gift of $500,000 rather than a current fund "participatory" gift of $25. Numbers of donors are not the answer for motivating probable healing results and cures. Numbers of dollars invested to accelerate resolution *is* the answer.

Motivation toward potential commitments is stimulated by the cited costs of cure. If those costs reflect probable results, it is similar to enjoying the demonstration of a great Mercedes, or Jaguar, or top Cadillac. But if the costs project results of a VW, we must look under the hood to see if a motor exists. Here the evidences of confidence will determine philanthropic results.

I have seen so much malarky proposed by administrative, medical, and professional staff just to get a buck that one must doubt the ethics and values of what is proposed as pathways to resolution.

Recently, a friend reported an organization's research efforts over four decades. Almost countless grants have been made for research scholars, fellows, fellowships, interns, and major researchers. I asked, "Who puts the findings and results together to avoid redundance, to see elements of progress, to cite benchmarks of progress?" He did not know, yet he was an insider! What an investment waste! Still, multitudes of small donors keep on investing in hope. It's like my experience several years ago when I visited a cancer organization and everyone was smoking cigarettes!

Today, motivation for greater and greater philanthropic productivity is stimulated by high-tech videos, films, radio, television, advertising, and news of tragedies in foreign countries. The question becomes, "Are we being over-motivated?" Such over-motivation can result in closure — closure of the heart and soul to do something.

Then we are deluged with direct mail over and over again. This becomes a physical and emotional harassment adding only to the volume in trash dumps. This fact is constantly being denied by volumes of uncertified statistics.

Yet, we can study all the motivation criteria in human psychology, physiology, sociology, and theology, and we must be students of those criteria as values toward which to strive. Strategic planning, at the same time, must adhere to the marketing ethics and values of "sales presentations" to potential investors who can make a difference.

Potential prospects look for evidence of good management, sound policies, moral communications, and ethical procedures as conditions precedent to other motivations of personal interests and concerns.

Administrators and volunteers must never prejudge the prospect's potential interest in their project because of their knowing the prospect's other interests. No one has the right to prejudge the prospect's interest to ever make a difference. Give him or her an ideal goal to achieve. The prospect will decide.

The presentation of invisible values as investment goals to insure such values requires the highest caliber of artistic preparation and presentation of values to touch the heart and soul of the prospect. Potential investors must be brought from just awareness, to interest, to concern, to commitment to make a difference. They alone can and will assess their values, then share those values with organizations who can multiply personal values many times for others.

Organizations themselves are philanthropies. They exist for the love of humankind to meet human needs and enhance human values.

Motivation is an intangible process of moving people from where they are resting to onward and upward levels of personal satisfaction for their own worth.

Personal values can be assured, even insured, only through motivating humanitarian philanthropy.

The Artistry of Giving

The act of being philanthropic — writing a check, signing a statement of intent, transferring securities and real estate, creating planned gift instruments, preparing bequests — each, all, and more must result from an inner will to share personal resources. What is the inner motivation to do what one is not required to do? What inner vision of accomplishment exists to require externalization? Love of humankind? Deep personal care? Gratitude? Pride? Ego?

What causes the visual or performing artist, the musician, the ballerina, the producer/director, the writer to create what has not yet been created? There must exist an inner yearning to express an idea, an ideal, a vision, a spiritual ministry, or a quiet, anonymous expression of love wherefrom I came, here I am, and further I go.

The expression of philanthropy is an art form, not just a series of mechanical happenings. Let's look at the instruments of the visual arts for comparisons:

First, the artists must have an *idea,* a *vision* of what to create and how to express that creation. The philanthropist must have an idea of what a gift will create, sustain, enhance or insure. First a spot on the canvas (a small gift), then full realization of that inner desire for consummate expression.

Then, the artist requires *tools* — raw materials, brush, pen, knife, and deft hands (mouth and feet as with handicapped artists). The activation tools applied to the potential philanthropist is the resource development volunteer and staff who as *investment counsellors* apply means of communication to motivate and inspire volunteer investments of the new or renewed philanthopist.

The visual artist requires a *canvas* to sketch the outlines of a picture, a sculpture. To the investment counsellor, the canvas is the case or prospectus — the picture of the mission and the vision of the organization's future. The canvas must yearn to be the basis of what is to be created.

On the canvas the *sketch* is the ultimate reality of the vision. Here, the soon to be born or reborn is the design to encourage personal, even anonymous, ownership of the vision to sustain or enhance investment ownership in the birth of the ultimate vision. Here the current fund gift takes form as the beginning of the impact of the inner will visualized.

The *medium* consists of the instruments for creating the ultimate art form — to draw, to form, to evolve. So it is with the investment counsellors to study, research, and study again the prospective philanthropist in preparation for promising the reality of interests, concerns, hopes, fears, ideals, and experiences before suggesting specific goals for investment.

The process of art is *application* — doing it. Here the true inspiration of the artist is revealed, combining talent, skill, understanding, and dreams. In the process of achieving philanthropic success, there are a series of prospect orientation, cultivation, and involvement options and the application of artful solicitation situations to inspire unprecedented philanthropy.

The result of the artist's work is *accomplishment* — the spirit of the artist revealed! To the philanthropist, there has been a voluntary investment in an intangible vision, a small step to insure a positive destiny forever serving humankind. The philanthropist has been educated along the way about how to invest, using available resources to bless himself/herself, the family, the heirs, and the organization.

The Process of Giving

Let's analyze the process. The process may be called the **psychological sequence of success** in philanthropic productivity. First, there must be *awareness* of the organization.

The prospect must be or must become *interested* in the organization. Prospect research procedures can reveal the prospect's depth of interests and concerns relative to the value of the organization to society.

Then, the prospect must be *involved* to accelerate and to deepen interest. The prospect's evidence of *concern* is next. Here the prospect may accept a volunteer position, become a current donor, host a community meeting, and on and on. Then comes *commitment.* Here the prospect becomes a substantial investor of time, talent, and treasure, none to the exclusion of the others. For some individuals and families, this process may require only 30 days to see positive results; for others, 30 years.

What then are the expectations for philanthropic investment results?

1. The mission is assured and reassured as viable, responsible, needed, and succeeding.
2. The goals of service to humankind are fair, understandable, implementable, and necessary to fulfill the mission.
3. The objectives of each goal are reasonable management and administrative processes as evaluated *every* six months.
4. The vision of service and philanthropic results are realized progressively and soundly.
5. Unprecedented philanthropic income for current operations, special projects, and endowment to assure — even insure — a sound, viable future.
6. The ministry of philanthropy has been found to be an art form applied by dedicated investment counsellors.

The artistry of giving results in applying the ministry of relating potential investors to opportunities for sharing diverse personal resources which they hold in trust for others.

The art of giving lies in capitalizing on diverse resources of personal income, a portion of estate resources for special projects currently, entering into deferred gift instruments, and including charities in final estate plans for a philanthropic impact for humankind.

What every living human being has and holds
is a temporary trust account gained to share.

Recall the greatest philanthropist the world has ever known and who has been unheralded as *the* greatest philanthropist. No one has ever gone on welfare in our society because of what he or she gave away. The widow thrived with no resources. We withhold for fear of need. The widow had no fear. She had faith and she shared without being asked.

Please read chapter 19 in the book *The Prophet* by Kahil Gibran.

The artistry of giving lives within every investment counsellor. No art; no result.

Thriving, Not Merely Surviving

Mere survival of our not-for-profit organizations is unacceptable as a management virtue. Maintaining the status quo guarantees obsolescence. Administrative or service crises stand as an indictment of management. Today, our society looks for evidence of stability and security amid evidence of growth with confidence.

Our philanthropic organizations and institutions today are launching unprecedented marketing programs and succeeding. These programs are designed for fiscal stability and security. At the same time, governing boards are retaining investment counsellors for highest possible productivity of their endowment resources. And constituents are providing greater and greater resource commitments in terms of goals being sought.

Today, philanthropic gift programs must be designed for donor results first. No one can predict with any exactitude the deep personal motivation of donors in the selection of gift objectives important to them. Therefore, a comprehensive resource development program must be designed to motivate concurrent gifts for budgeted purposes, for special programs and services, for equipment and physical facilities, and for endowed fiscal stability and security for ongoing as well as for unexpected financial needs.

Successful and generous philanthropic productivity must be designed. That design must be comprehensive to inform constituents of diverse financial requirements of the facility and to stimulate constituent interest to invest in those features important to them. All proposed programs should be couched in investment terms — investments in the maintenance and enhancement of all services.

Gifts of Confidence

Yes, I have recommended the closure of three organizations to prevent the harassment of their constituents whose confidence in them wavered seriously.

When such a organization is confronted by a variety of negatives — service, annual support, weak board members and staff, and other disappointments, confidence wanes even citing probable closure.

There was one institution, however, on the brink of financial stress which had a most unusual governing board. It was unusual because of the composition of its membership. Cash flow was the problem. The competent resource development personnel only sought minimal gifts as participants, not necessarily investments, to ensure quality from these members.

I interviewed each board member to ascertain their concept of their role, function, responsibility, and obligation to ensure thriving, not just survival, of the organization. Nearly every person reported their doubt that the institution could survive, even though its services were critical to the community and region.

The weight of probable recommendations were heavy. Yet, there in that board alone lay enormous current, special project, and endowment potential. The first problem — the first financial potential lay in that board. A sense of frustration and disappointment permeated the entire institution.

Then, the right occasion presented itself. I was to be at a debriefing dinner at the home of the chief development officer, the chief executive officer and his wife, the board chairman and his wife, and the board development committee chairman and his wife. There was the usual refreshment hour.

When all left the room to be seated at the dining table, only the board chairman and I failed to rise. Here was a man of incredible community stature. He was not related to the institution except as a private citizen concerned with its needed community service.

I cited to him the persistent fear and expectancy that the institution would have to close. I cited to him that the first potential lay in the heart, hands, and resources of board members first. I cited the urgency and necessity to reach board members for unprecedented "gifts of confidence" to the institution of $100,000 each for each of five years. I named 10 such trustees and asked him to be the first member for such a commitment (no one in that town had ever given $500,000 to any charity ever).

The chairman was stunned and intrigued. He said that he would do it. We adjourned to the dining room but he couldn't eat. He told of my recommendation while the others ate.

The next day he began his one-on-one appointments with board members. There was no case. There were no forms. All gifts were to be anonymous but verified to him in writing.

He saw seven of the 10. With himself there were five commitments of $500,000 and two of $100,000 each. He announced this early result at an executive committee meeting of the board. Those $2,700,000 worth of Gifts of Confidence made headlines in the next day's paper.

All, repeat, all attitudes changed. All expectancies changed. Later there was a $32,000,000 asset-building program created and staffed by staff. Other organizations in town, too, began receiving six- and seven-figure gifts.

Gifts of Confidence work. But the governing board did it as governing boards must — properly designed, properly composed of diverse competencies, properly led, and properly staffed.

The chairman became a hero in "selling" investments in the institution at a level of fiscal substance to spark the assurance of academic quality. Persons of influence and/or affluence must be presented with philanthropic motivations to stimulate their desire and capacity to make a difference, not levels "to just get by."

Confidence, pure and simple, is one unsung motivational
factor underlying the probability of success of all philanthropic
programs.

Personal Rewards of Sharing Through Caring

Most people would laugh at the suggestion that giving a piece
of property to a charity could result in greater inheritance for heirs.
But it is true. One college had over 200 farms coming to it which
the heirs do not want to occupy or to deal with as an inheritance.
One museum had two beautiful, classic, large residences given to
it. Their heirs feel the same way. Present occupants live in these
properties through two lives and receive current federal gift tax
deducation benefits for their gift of their deed. Too, the occupant's
estate taxes will be reduced because the property is no longer a
part of the estate; therefore, the estate is in a lower federal estate
tax bracket. The donors, the heirs, and the philanthropies benefit.
The heirs are surprised, relieved, and impressed that they benefit
because of what was invested in philanthropies which they never
thought would help them, too. Their attitudes about giving and
sharing and caring changed to positive actions on their own
behalf. Those heirs now become prospects to honor their parents
in a meaningful way out of a strong sense of gratitude.

Not too long ago there was massive publicity about the children and heirs of nationally recognized affluent persons. Those
young people are engaged — even engrossed — in diverse philanthropies as leaders and donors. They learned their responsibilities, pleasures, obligations, and opportunities from their parents.

Now in process with one client is the establishment of a
wealth replacement trust whereby property is set aside in a
separate trust, the value of which goes to a philanthropy. Its tax
gift deduction is used in part to acquire a special life insurance
policy in the amount of the property value. The insurance policy
beneficiaries are the client's heirs who do not have to pay taxes

on the policy's income. The net benefit to them someday is far greater than expected had that property not been given away. They want to learn more about this mystique called philanthropy.

Malcom S. Forbes gave Princeton University the cost of a new building to be named for his son and probable heir to his magazine and fortune. The son cannot help being impressed to "go thou and do likewise."

All philanthropic investors are models for future imitation, but we must bring families into the appreciation process insofar as possible. Heirs of present investors should be followed as future prospects for honoring their parents' ministry of caring for others.

One staff investment counsellor stopped asking people for money or other resources for various gift objectives. Through intensive prospect research and frequent visits under various auspices, he learned much about people's families and business affairs. He knew their hobbies, concerns, eccentricities, and care about his college.

When the time was right, he would visit them to talk about their ideals, dreams, hopes, and concerns in life and in the future of their children's and grandchildren's society. He made it clear that he was not there to ask for a gift. Rather, he wanted to ask them a question about which they may never have thought. That question was: "If you had all the resources possible, what in your lifetime would you like to see accomplished? A professorship in theology, art, engineering, law? A building dedicated to someone? Adequate funds to insure a college education for deserving youth? Endowment of all administrative expenses of an organization? What would you like to see ensured?"

The prospects would be stunned by the magnitude and import of the question. They would discuss dreams and ideals together for the first time. After a while he would leave to let them think about the question. He would seek an appointment in two or three weeks to talk again. They would see him because of their interest and concern for the initial question. After some discussion, he would say that there is nothing about which you can dream that cannot be accomplished in microcosm at our college. Then he would discuss options for realizing their dream at his college. He would show them how to invest now and plan for investments later, to see their dream in action now and insured later.

The results of this ministry were astounding. Many, many individuals and families became substantial philanthropists beyond their wildest dreams.

He discovered their values. He built upon their values the opportunity to achieve great, great personal satisfaction in being able to accomplish the impossible. He used the tools of philanthropy to build reality out of a dream.

So don't just ask for money. Don't insult your prospect or your organization as a beggar asking for a buck. Train yourself, your trustees, your staff associates, and your volunteers that, as investment counsellors, you are not taking anything away from them or their family. In fact, you are providing perpetual opportunities to achieve spiritual satisfaction beyond human estimation through investing for the benefit of others.

Recognize that you do not know the deep personal concerns of your prospects and their families by showing them all the things that can be accomplished through their decisions for endowments from $10,000 to $25,000,000. Then show them how easy it is today to provide $1,000,000 conveniently and at low cost.

One trustee of a client institution obtained a life insurance policy on his 22-year-old son for $1,000,000. It cost him some $4,000 for six years. That's all. The son, too, is an investor.

With another client, we had three prospects interested in providing $5,000,000 charitable life insurance policies each together with market fund provisions which would provide the philanthropy in 20 to 30 years a $1,000,000 income forever. This new technique is called **capitalized philanthropy.**

Today, philanthropic impact can be substantial, but organization investment counsellors need not be technicians. They must be strategists.

But to achieve unprecedented financial stability and security for our deserving organizations, those organizations must get their whole act together in accelerating and enhancing their ministry of philanthropy to their constituents.

There must be creditable, authenticating governing board leadership. There must be an organizational design for its destiny together with anticipated costs. There must be highly respected administrative leadership. There must be an investment counsellor staff with great talent for creativity. There must be strong advocacy for the organization. There must be confidence in the management of resources. And prospects must be presented with diverse investment gift objectives and options for their achievement.

Your constituents exist. They are ready to respond. Are you really ready to show them and their families how to share their caring?

Successful philanthropy is the by-product of good management.

Million-Dollar Donors: Their Problems and Your Potential

If you had the innate desire, the opportunity or the mandate to give away one million dollars, by what system of analysis would you decide to give it? All at once? Ten gifts of $100,000 each? Twenty gifts of $50,000 each? Two gifts of $500,000?

To what charitable organization or organizations would you provide the gift? By what criteria? By whose criteria?

How would your prejudices influence your preferences? If you solicit requests for all or some of the fund, how would you judge the efficacy of those requests? How do you judge the requesting organization's validity of need, proof of the wise management of resources, their studied priorities as objective and valid, or the certainty of their destiny? How would you stimulate the greatest impact of their gift? By multiplying the beneficial effect of their gift or gifts through a challenge offer? Or is this not a legitimate aim of philanthropy?

Would you request that their gift or gifts be applied to operating expenses; to physical plant building or maintenance; to special projects or programs; or to temporary or permanent endowment? Would the award be unrestricted, designated or for budgeted purposes, or legally restricted as to purpose?

Would you try to obtain some return on your "investment" through a life tenancy agreement on your residence, farm, ranch or resort property; a charitable gift annuity; pooled income fund; or other deferred gift device?

How do you decide all of these things? To whom do you look for experienced advice? A committee? A special counsellor? Probable recipients? A counsellor inexperienced in the complexities of third-party philanthropic gifts? A bank trust officer trained as a conservator of wealth rather than one who plans for sharing wealth? Or one never concerned for self-gain or gain for business reasons but one experienced in the philosophy, the spirit and the techniques of philanthropy — the trained development officer or planned giving officer of potential recipient organizations? Yes, technical specialists are required for the *final, technical* preparation of documents required by state authorities and Internal Revenue Service personnel.

No, it is not easy to give away a million dollars or more. Each such donor must go through some series of questions as those cited. It is interesting to recall an extensive study of donors of million-dollar gifts some years ago. In that study, donors revealed that the first of 12 elements of consideration in deciding to make that gift was "self-generated conviction." In other words, the donor initiated the idea of the gift to its recipient organization! (Incidentally, tax considerations was fifth of those 12.) Other elements? Objectives of the organization and plans to meet them. Efficiency of the organization. Competence of the organization's leadership. Needs of the organization. Regular reports on how funds are used. Personal solicitation by a volunteer or friend. Follow-up each year. Perpetuating a family name. Mailed request. Public appeal. These are real-life reactions by those who gave.

What will never be known are the thought processes: the inner spiritual motivations for the sharing of resources; the analyses of perceptions of the organization; the impressions of the leadership and authenticating quality of the governing board; the tender loving care in invitations to special events; the sensitive care of members of the family; the way telephone operators answer phones, the way secretaries who reply "Mr. Who?" and more — observations which cause persons of substantial resources to offer to share them.

The study cited above also contains a shrouded indictment of organizational managers. If donors who provide gifts of one million dollars or more cite that the decision was the result of "self-generated conviction," could it be that the individual was not asked to provide that sum in the first place? This happens more often than we would like to have studied and analyzed further. Staff members, officers, trustees, and volunteers are too often intimidated by persons of wealth in terms of giving them the oppportunity to provide a gift commensurate with the prospect's estimate of the prospect's interest, concern, and capacity. Further, these same organizational persons are so overcome by obtaining numbers of donors that 90 percent of time and 90 percent budget are given to small donor productivity. Those who could have a truly remarkable impact on the organization get "short shrift," requesting only "participatory" gifts in $1,000 clubs. What would happen — what could happen — if the percentage figures were reversed to give 90 percent of time to that one percent to five percent of constituents who could have such an impact as to affect the destiny of the organization possibly forever?

In spite of all the current doom-and-gloom talk about the reduction of philanthropic gift growth, the real problem in gift growth lies within the organization's prospect priorities to reach and motivate potential donors to assist in catapulting the organization to new levels of philanthropic achievement.

If you had one million dollars in diverse resources to give away, what questions would you seek to answer to be absolutely certain that, among the thousands and thousands of worthy organizations, the one you selected would husband those resources for maximum organization impact? Transfer your present position to that of a person on your prospect list for whom research and study shows that such potential exists. Would you give your one million to your present organization — the one you serve? What are the missing elements of confidence which must be corrected to win your financial commitment? Personal interests, personalities, and personal prejudices aside, organizational philanthropic fund raising personnel must be able to "sell" their organization with the same confidence as if they were the prospect being solicited. (Of course, they must also be donors first, each to the extent of personal capacity plus generosity born of personal commitment.)

Organizational personnel responsible for management of services, programs, personnel, plant, equipment, and finances must be conscious of those criteria affecting or likely to affect the favorable response from those to whom they look for generous, continuing, and increasing financial support. This does not mean at all that potential donors must dictate in any way the nature of such management imperatives. It does mean that there is a cause and effect relationship in addition to the rampant disinclination to take the time to study, to woo, and to win unprecedented support from those who have the capacity to affect the destiny of the organization.

The organization must also be prepared to indicate options to the million-dollar prospect. Each reader could present a list of such options, but here's a starter:

1. an unrestricted, undesignated endowment fund, the income from which will be applied as needed;
2. endowment of the chief executive office, thus removing it, in fact, from the budget;
3. endowment for equipment obsolescence;
4. immediate utilization for crucial maintenance too long deferred, for fire safety, for handicapped persons, for roof and window repairs to conserve energy and the plant itself;
5. endowment for furnishings and vehicle replacement;
6. endowment for computerization of administrative records and procedures;
7. a three-year challenge to increase annual support from all constituents or from individual sources only;
8. an endowment challenge to governing board members only;
9. endowment for library, audio, and video acquisitions;
10. endowment for publications necessary for constituency motivations;
11. endowment for services to needy students, patients, clients, etc.;
12. named departments or staff positions;
13. expenditure for external physical plant improvement — landscaping, signs, lights, etc.;
14. endowment for visiting lecturers, scientists, scholars, artists, businessmen, politicians, professionals, etc.;

15. endowment for professional staff development for academic degrees, enhancement of status, publications, etc.;
16. underwriting the relations and financial support budgets for three to five years as appropriate;
17. underwriting the fringe benefit program of organizational personnel;
18. alternation of physical plant facilities;
19. provide a residence for the chief executive and endowment for its maintenance;
20. leadership incentive gift for a low-key, high gift level, sophisticated capital fund program;
21. endowment for existing physical plant units or features — lobbies, offices, auditorium, laboratories, whole buildings, residence facilities, etc.;
22. endowment for research, special projects;
23. endowment for awards, public events, etc.; and,
24. funds for other budget items, the endowment of which frees funds for other uses.

Prospective donors need ideas for thoughtful philanthropy — ideas that trigger ideals, concerns, interests, nostalgia. Such well prepared tabulations of gift opportunities can serve as inspiration to potential donors to contemplate and resolve either for immediate gifts or for inclusion in bequests or estate plans.

At the same time, organizational personnel should prepare formats about how to give one million dollars. Cash is not the only answer. Multiple resources should be anticipated, including securities; transfers of existing life insurance no longer needed; gifts of stock in newly-formed corporations; oil, mineral, patent, and copyrights; collections of coins and stamps; creating new life insurance; creation of charitable lead trusts, annuities, pooled income funds; and other personal or business resources. Which ones must be relegated to a fiduciary agent? What does your officially approved gifts and grants policy state? To be able to seek a million-dollar gift, the organization must be prepared to present options and have the capability to assure potential donors of the confidence in the organization that it can manage such gifts.

There is no dearth of prospective donors of gifts of a million dollars or more. It was not too long ago that a government agency revealed that there were more than 500,000 individuals with annual incomes of a million dollars or more and that women exceeded men in this category. Who are these persons within your constituent orbit? Are you prepared to give them the opportunity, with confidence, they seek in their own desire and need for personal fulfilment in helping others substantially philanthropically?

If your organization does not, another one will.

How to Give a Million Dollars

Not long ago, there was a man in Michigan who had a dream, a deeply rooted desire, to provide a gift of a million dollars. But he didn't have a million dollars. He was "comfortably fixed," as the saying goes. So he began to ask how can one provide a million-dollar philanthropic gift without having a million dollars in cash or other resources. He found one way.

He got his 40-year-old son to agree that his life be insured for one million dollars but that the sole beneficiary be a preferred charitable organization. The premium for his son's life insurance would be far less than the premium for himself, assuming that he was insurable. So a life insurance policy was secured, delivered to the charity as sole beneficiary with half of the 11-year term policy premiums paid by the charity and half by his own resources. The charity was pleased for the small investment to be assured on one million dollars. The donor got a personal gift tax deduction for his premium payments. His son was gratified that his father found a way to realize a dream. Everyone was pleased. Everyone benefited.

Moral: You must first *want* to give a million dollars deeply in your heart. Second, you must seek out a comfortable way for your personal and family interests and reasonably achievable from your available resources.

People do not consider providing truly generous gifts solely from the gift tax deductibility standpoint. A study among seven- and eight-figure donors found that tax considerations were eighth in a list of 16 considerations for providing such gifts. Confidence in the management of the receiving institution was number one.

Those who cannot give a million-dollar gift achieve the same personal and spiritual fulfillment for having had a significant impact on the receiving organization by providing a gift of a lesser amount. A gift of $100,000 or $250,000 or $500,000 can be worth a million to the donor in quiet, personal satisfaction for having accomplished a great goal. To those who can think and plan beyond the one-million-dollar level, perhaps their "impact" gift could be $1,500,000 or $2,500,000 or $5,000,000 or $10,000,000 or more. People can and do give at these levels and achieve quiet, personal satisfaction.

Quiet, personal satisfaction? How come, when such gifts are given just to have the donor's name on things? Not so, absolutely not! Again, studies have shown that most great philanthropic gifts are anonymous or are for internal organization knowledge only. It is the organizational solicitors who persuade such donors to place their names up front as an example for others "to go thou and do likewise." Of course, such philanthropy is a source of gratification to all concerned, which can take many forms for recognition of the gift.

No one "has" to give personal resources away. But some portion of those resources can be combined into diverse devices thereby capitalizing upon, first the desire and, second, the means to accomplish what was heretofore considered to be impossible.

There are many kinds of financial counsellors who can provide confidential help in designing diverse means to achieve philanthropic goals once personal interests are determined:

- First, planned giving personnel on the staffs of charitable organizations should be the first persons consulted about how, for what purpose, by what means, etc., such gifts may be considered. They are on salary; they receive no commissions or fees on what they recommend. They represent no financial profession though some may be attorneys. They represent the charity only in helping prospects to assist that charity. They are true specialists in planning how to use personal resources to accomplish the organization's mission and goals. Recommended alternatives would next be tested with personal legal, banking or other counsellors to be sure that state and federal rules and regulations apply for short-term and long-term protection of the family and that of the charity itself.

- Second, a new counselling service is called estate planning counsellors. Here, informed, experienced specialists give 100 percent of their time to help people plan their personal financial security objectives. However, seldom, if ever, do they show how clients and their heirs can benefit by being philanthropic and still maintain their own financial security. So each person must initiate discussions by suggesting that they want to help their church, education or health care institution, art museum, etc., and still secure family interests and retirement years.

- Third, attorneys who, by virtue of their certified credentials, are *presumed* to be expert in all phases of legal counselling. Many are not such experts. There are legal specialists who are truly objective and experienced in all of the diverse deferred giving devices. Therefore, each potential donor must look beyond *general* counsellors to truly capable specialists in estate planning who first are concerned about client interests.

- Fourth, trust officers of banking institutions whose function is to counsel as well as to promote banking interests. Potential donors who desire to provide maximum benefit to preferred charities and have resources left for their families and for themselves should seek out banking institutions with large trust departments having a variety of estate specialists rather than the so-called "friendly corner banker."

- Fifth, among those personal counsellors available to help plan philanthropic gift objectives are life insurance, real estate, investment, and accounting executives. These professionals are in a position to counsel on gifts relating to their respective services. However, very, very seldom are they called upon for advice in philanthropic areas and are not always able to provide safe advice on the features and factors of complex gifts of life insurance, real property, securities or other resources.

- Sixth and last among available counsellors for the philanthropic disposition of assets are staff officers of community trusts or community foundations. These fiduciary vehicles are repositories of assets for either recurring or eventual disposition of resources placed in their hands. Donors have the right and responsibility to indicate how their resources shall be distributed to one or more charities. Usually when such assets are placed in such community funds, the donor doubts the capacity of the receiving charity to produce the investment income amount which can be instead achieved through the management of large endowment sums.

Having sought the best possible advice and preferably second and third options on what investment gift objectives the preferred charity needs and can use consistent with the donor's interest, what are the options to consider? Some of these options follow, but the suggestions listed below should not be considered all-inclusive:

I. Gifts of cash.

a. One check of $1,000,000.
b. Checks of $200,000 each for five years; $100,000 for each year for 10 years; $500,000 in each of two years.
c. Annual gifts of $100,000 figured at 10 percent on an endowment amount of $1,000,000 to be provided by bequest.
d. Gifts of cash plus deed of residence, farm, ranch, resort, or commercial property to reach $1,000,000.
e. Gifts of cash plus beneficiary transfer of existing or new life insurance.
f. Gift provided for by bequest or estate plan with statement of intent provided now.

II. Gifts of securities.

a. Ownership transfer of appreciated securities. Gift amount is the value on date of transfer and delivery to charity.

b. Sale of securities on which there is a loss to take deduction for the loss and then the gift of proceeds to charity.
c. Gifts of securities in new business ventures.
d. These options plus those of No. 1 above.

III. Gifts of life insurance.

a. Gifts of present life insurance no longer needed for heirs whether insurance is paid up or not. Premiums on insurance are tax deductible annually only after the charity is named owner of the policy and the beneficiaries are changed by the insurance company with the policy delivered to the charity.
b. Gifts of new life insurance with the charity designated owner and beneficiary and delivered to the charity after which premiums are tax deductible.
c. Naming a charity as beneficiary of life insurance taken out by employer with premiums paid by employer. This form is most available in non-public firms.

IV. Gifts of real estate.

a. Gifts of residence, farm or ranch now with life occupancy retained by donor. Deed is made out and delivered to charity now. Gift credit and tax deduction reflects the market value of property and the value of the occupancy to the donor.
b. Gifts of commercial property; vacant land; portions of land; oil, gas, mineral rights.

V. Charitable lead trust.

This trust is a means whereby parents or grandparents can transfer resources to charity for a period of more than 10 years, income is received by the named charity after which period of years the corpus reverts to children or grandchildren free of most taxes: estate, gift, etc.

There are other forms of this trust, but this form is most popular and appealing to grandparents.

VI. Various trusts.

These must be investigated with respected, experienced counsellors in terms of donor income preferences as well as gift preferences. These include but are not limited to unitrusts, annuity, and remainder trusts.

Herein lie diverse techniques which together or in combination offer donors the opportunity for truly great philanthropy. What are the steps in providing a million-dollar gift?

Step 1.   Decide that you wish to provide the greatest gift possible for a gift objective and a charity important to you. Without that deep desire, the process and the event and the personal reward will not happen.

Step 2.   Select a gift opportunity — a goal. These can include a charity's program; project; service; an officer or staff position; an office or department function; equipment or library acquisition; a building unit, endowment of present or new building, or landscape beautification; or unrestricted endowment which is always preferred by every charity.

Step 3.   Contact the charity's chief executive officer to ascertain if the preferred gift objective is desired and available. If it is, reserve it pending final arrangements.

Step 4.   Contact the charity's planned gift officer to ascertain board-approved gift options and discuss how those options meet your gift capacity.

Step 5.   Affirm preferred gift options with broadly experienced estate planning legal counsel.

Step 6. Notify charity of the decision and method of giving to reserve the preferred gift opportunity requesting confidentiality as an anonymous or publicly acknowledged present or eventual donor.

How to give a million dollars? The idea must be born out of a deep sense of personal gratitude for resources received, for benefits of the receiving charity in serving mankind, to insure the charity's services in perpetuity, to perpetuate one's life interests or commitments to recognize or memorialize loved ones or those who affected the donor's life of because of man's concern for our fellow human beings.

Investment gift opportunities are without limit in number. The means for achieving personal desires are diverse. The opportunity to act is now. The time to act is now before it is too late. The will to act is in your heart and hands.

๑๔ 4 ๖๏
The Management
of Process

*Successful philanthropy ought to be the by-product of
good management and good administration.*

*In this age of uncertainty there are no shortcuts
to fiscal viability.*

The essential elements for successful philanthropy include the
case or prospectus (a compelling opportunity for donors/
investors to accomplish something important), constituency
(people and organizations who care about the case), leadership (volunteers and a CEO who have the personal power to
take the case to the constituency), and lastly organization
(staff, tools, events).

Organization is not what is ultimately important — you
don't begin with organization — but there can be no successful
gift income program without it. Organization — bureaucracy
and brochures and plans — should be low profile, visible only
enough to give leadership and donors confidence that the
institution is being well run. Organization usually gets noted
when it malfunctions — then it becomes terribly important. So
a review of some of the principles and tactics is appropriate.

105

The Role of Resource Development

Successful fund development programs result from carefully planned steps designing an institution's destiny, retaining sensitive and creative administrators, and lastly, creating a system of persuasion with evidence to earn the confidence of all constituencies. Success in the entire resource development function affects every sequential function.

The development professional must possess 15 essential characteristics, features which never appear on sterile resumes:

1. one who has sales-oriented instincts;
2. one capable of developing the art of prospect cultivation and persuasion;
3. one who is or who will become a student of the philosophy and psychology of philanthropy;
4. one who possesses creative energy and initiative;
5. one who cares about all the diverse motivations of potential donors;
6. one who is articulate in the written and spoken expository word;
7. one who sets work habit models for staff, peers, and volunteers alike;
8. one whose poise, dress, and habits depict accepted norms of executive behavior;
9. one who takes pride in communication to peers and staff alike;
10. one who is never satisfied with the status quo in designs for persuasion or process;
11. one who demonstrates the worthwhileness of the sales process by sharing personal resources generously first;
12. one who seeks advice and takes it as well as gives it;
13. one who obtains personal satisfaction in the joy and accolades reaped upon others;
14. one who is sensitive to providing well written, comprehensive data and assistance to help others look good on behalf of the institution; and
15. one who is an attentive listener.

These are very personal traits. Except for a few, they are never acquired. Those who cannot measure up to the talent and skills required for expected progress and success, should seek happiness and rewards elsewhere before damage is done to personal reputations or to the organization. Not everyone should devote precious years to a position or field unless there is a deep personal satisfaction achieved.

Now let us turn to what confronts this eager, talented paraprofessional in the successful culmination of an awaiting career.

The role of philanthropic resource development is best explained in a diagrammatic agenda. The following sequence cites all factors required for successful productivity if increasingly generous philanthropy is desired:

$$\frac{A(B/S)+P(A/F)+N/O+Adm}{Cs+P(r)+Cu/Co+V+Ask} \times CR \frac{Pr+Pi}{(C+Pu)}$$

$$\times CDP \frac{A+C+P}{(S+B)} \times S/G = \$S(s/s)$$

This coded agenda has been developed through nearly 50 years of experience in observing failures and success in program planning, in staff and volunteer implementation, in donor generosity and disappointments, in powerful and powerless trustee and volunteer enlistment, and in recognition of and disregard of prospect motivation.

This agenda constitutes a state-of-readiness platform, the analysis of which, predetermines the general timeliness and feasibility of various programs, mandated preconditions and positioning, as well as staff and program criteria.

A simplified, interpretative version of this agenda looks like this:

$$\frac{Positioning}{Preparation} \times Promotion \times Production = Product$$

In this abstract, only a very brief description of the agenda will be provided. A separate session can be built around each symbol and code designation.

"A" means authenticators; governing board members, "B"; and support groups, "S" such as alumni, members, patients, and audiences; parents and families; businesses, counsellors and other groups of volunteer persons. Here, in summary, the state-of-readiness analyst looks for evidences of power among individual members — power by reason of position, of influence, of affluence. The analyst also looks for evidence of generous contributions of both time and multiple financial resources (as appropriate) as commitments of confidence and acceptance of leadership responsibility.

"P" stands for planning. Perhaps the letter should be "D" for destiny. The organization which has not systematically designed its future services and financial costs in terms of data on all issues, forces, and trends does not matter. It will not be here long. The "A" here stands for internal program and service planning; "F" for financial planning. The costs of quality, the costs of stability and security, not the costs of survival are crucial here. Thus, a five-year, documented plan, a vision for the future constitutes a design for organizational destiny. But there is more. . . .

The symbol "N" signifies needs — basic non-deferrable programmatic, equipment, facility, personnel, and financial needs representing operational, special capital, and endowment requirements. "O" signifies all extant gift opportunities available to potential donors beginning with those that can be endowed out of the budget; then those representing departments, divisions, programs, services, positions, and physical plant units; and finally those it would be nice to have. This is plain and simple merchandising of what already exists.

"ADM" stands for administration. All administrative persons and units must be a firm partnership and completely supportive of these elements for a certain destiny. As they share in the dreaming and the planning, they must share in the sensitive implementation of each advancement facet. This category includes executive and all staff members.

These above-the-line factors combine to "position" the organization for the success ultimately desired.

The below-the-line factors are the fund program preparation requirements.

Why anyone should give a dollar to the organization must be answered in a consensus-building, confidence-building case — "Ca." This should be considered a sales document, not an essay, theme, dissertation, or historic article. It is a sales document! And it is probably best accomplished and quickest by outside specialists who can see the forest *and* the trees. But there is more. . . .

"P(r)" is the symbol for crucial prospect identification and prospect research functions. All constituents are prospects for gifts and grants for budgeted operations *and* all individuals are prospects for an endowment bequest of some size even to endow their annual support. However, substantial gifts can be expected from some 10 percent of a given constituency with one to five percent of that constituency providing five-, six-, seven-, and eight-figure gifts. Hence, the crucial importance of prospect research as the most indispensable function of the entire fund development operation.

"Cu/Co" is the awkward symbol for prospect orientation, cultivation, and conference market-testing of the case with selected "suspects" and prospects. This process is intended to develop prospect interest, from apathy to involvement and commitment. For some prospects, this process requires many years; for others a matter of months. The "Co" symbol refers to the market-testing process of presenting the case to key persons in small groups for discussion of draft documents proposing motivational analyses for programs and projects.

"V" stands for the indispensable volunteer sales force — persons who can be trained to present investment opportunities to prospects for their philanthropic consideration. The volunteer corps should be no larger than the administrative staff can handle comfortably. The fewer well trained, experienced, able and eager volunteeres, the better. We do not want or need meer solicitors. We need investment advisors. But there is more. . . .

"Ask." Someone, sometime, in some manner must ask for the investment gift. Eyeball to eyeball, phone to phone, personal letter, direct mail — each and all has a role. But productivity will diminish in dollar size down from the personal, in-person request to direct mail. There is an art in the manner of presenting the investment request. Each prospect worthy of a personal visit should be asked to consider a range of investment gifts: First, suggest what is hoped for as a proud investment; then suggest an upper range thereby complimenting the prospect; then suggest a lower range. But always suggest that the gift commitment must be the prospect's personal decision in terms of confidence in the present and future plans of the organization and the manner and style of the person(s) requesting the investment.

Now we come to the conditioning features. Positioning the organization in each constituent's mind and heart is a constant process of constituency relations, "CR," involving the art of image making, image building, constituency-member-internal-community relations, communication "C," public relations "Pr," public information "Pi," and publication "Pu."

Constituency relations is an art of interpretation and presentation of the organization — placing it in perspective of its mission, its goals, its peers, its potential, its history, and its distinction. Each of these elements is designed to retain interest and priority support from present friends and donors and to attract the interest and commitment of new donors, new prospects, and media specialists.

Public relations is a function seldom practiced fully in most organizations. Usually this title is attributed to publications specialists only. Publications are but one vehicle in the public relations arena. Specialized communications, media exposure, speaker's bureau, audio-visual materials, special events, officer–staff speaking tours, musical and arts tours, special events — each and all are public relations tools for positioning the institution for requested constituency response. The end product of constituency relations — the general public; select families; businesses; foundations; organizations and associations as well as government agencies — should be greater understanding of the institution — its history, role, personalities, needs, priorities, potential; more and better programs and services; more powerful trustees and greater financial support.

All constituents should know that the organization knows its costs of assured and even enhanced quality offerings. They should be aware of its comprehensive management planning, projections, priorities, costs, and investment gift objectives. These should lay the foundation for confidence in the institution's leadership, its management ,its future. This foundation then serves as a platform for launching a comprehensive financial resource development program, "CDP."

Elements of such a program includes the current fund, "A," as the basic gift support program encouraging gifts from donor income to the organization's income for recurring and increasingly generous support; the special, capital and asset-building program, "C," for people, program, plant, and endowment needs primarily for budget-relieving objectives seeking support from capital or asset resources as well as grants; and a planned giving program, "P," seeking current gift commitments (in addition to annual fund commitments) for gift objectives to be endowed out of the budget through deferred gift devices. The title, planned giving program, is not a substitute for deferred giving program.

Staff, "S," and budget, "B," must be of sufficient capacity to insure the success expected. In smaller organizations, staff should be multi-talented and capable of administering time and designing program elements so as to accomplish desired results. Larger organizations can afford specialists, but care must be exercised by management imperatives to ensure productivity.

Even with all of these considerations, there must be time and productivity schedules, "S," established early in the fiscal year and dollar goals, "G," to meet and to beat.

This agenda, then, sets into motion with each element in various states of completion and implementation, should result in dollar, "$," achievement; membership support, "S," and financial stability, "s," and security, "s" earned and deserved.

Here, then, is the whole picture of the design and impact of the fund development function on the organization. No longer can any trustee, organization officer, staff member, friend or member look to the resource development office only as the panacea of their gripes, disappointments or financial woes.

The resource development job is everybody's job: to plan and to participate in consciousness-building, in confidence-building, and in contribution-building on the basis of sound management principles of governing boards implemented by staff persons of talent, dedication, and zeal for the highest professional accomplishment; more friends, better friends, more funds, more stability in service to others.

Mobilization of Philanthropic Resources

Today our nonprofit organizations have the opportunity to create far more sophisticated philanthropic resource development programs than those which were developed when I came into this field in 1948. Gradually our society has become more sophisticated in perceptions of the indispensability of our independent sector and the requirements for fiscal stability and security of that sector. Yet, the independent sector is dependently independent. Each organization counts more and more on its constituents and expects more of its constituents in order to thrive, not merely survive.

The mobilization of resource factors include the following:

1. Planning. Today, we have an enormous flow of demographic data, which, when applied to perspectives of an organization's future, can foretell probable points of stress and strain. Using such data in the planning process may help to avoid crises. It is possible to design an organization's destiny rather than wait for happenstance to affect that destiny. In 1948, there was no real planning. The excuse was that there were too many intangibles to assume and to weigh. We built, but without confidence of long-term eventualities.

2. Governance. Today, governing board membership is not an honor solely. It embodies deep personal commitments, obligations, and responsibilities for sound, productive management. Board composition and function must be prescribed by criteria, position descriptions, and evaluation by a board management committee. Governing board functions are prescribed by law as a public trust first under not-for-profit corporate statutes, of which very few members are aware.

3. Resource Potential. We recognize that our constituents have income resources for current (annual) fund objectives; investment resources for urgent capital fund requirements; and estate resources for endowment — none to the exclusion of others — from assets for asset-building.

We are aware, today, that business firms and general purpose foundations were not created to solve all philanthropic organizational problems. Neither were governments.

4. Endowment. Today, we are aware of the crucial role of endowment to serve as reserves for short-term as well as long-term fiscal stability and security. At the same time, we are aware of the urgency and necessity for such funds to be managed by highly experienced investment counselling firms.

5. Marketing. Today, we are aware of the remarkable opportunity to "merchandise" our programs, services, personnel, budgeted features and functions (and those not budgeted) as both current fund and endowment investments to insure the future.

Our gift level club programs create continuity of support through membership attribution, but we fail to suggest that these memberships, at least, be endowed for perpetual impact and donor fulfillment. "Life members" means giving for life.

6. Resource Development. The fund-raising function, today, is viewed as a joint, administrative, team role wherein the resource development officer is viewed as the "sales manager" but not the star salesperson. Too, the productivity function is related to all management preconditions of governing board leadership; other volunteer groups; the planning process; public relations/ public information/communications functions; prospect research and prospect orientation.

7. Personnel. Today, personnel in the resource development function are accepted as executives, rather than clerks, trained by experience in the art of resource development at the highest possible productivity levels.

Crucial in augmenting this state of executive capacity has been the diverse programs, workshops, and seminars by various associations and the indispensable Fund Raising School now part of the Center for Philanthropy of Indiana University in Indianapolis.

8. Psychology. Today, far greater understanding and respect of human motivations for philanthropic generosity exists in terms of why people give; and why they don't. There are two indispensable publications (one book and one article) which every CEO, governing board member, resource development staff person, and some select volunteers should have: *Mega Gifts* by Jerold Panas (Bonus Books, Inc., 1984) and "Seeking a Godly Perspective for Fund Raisers," by Wesley K. Willmer (*Fund Raising Management*, July 1987).

9. Planned Giving. Today, only six percent of all individual gifts are by bequest. However, this figure will increase three to five times because of the massive effort being expended under auspices of planned giving programs in showing people how to give to benefit the organization of their choice, themselves, their estate, and their heirs. Showing people how to give — how to be philanthropic investors — is and will be the most vital philanthropic productivity function short-term and long-term.

These are all conditions that precede to high philanthropic productivity today and tomorrow. Every comprehensive resource development program should have the following format:

PHASE I. Current Operations. $ _____

A named current fund program to insure balanced budgets increasing 10 percent annually for unrestricted and designated gifts but never bequest income.

PHASE II. Urgent, non-deferrable objectives. $ _____

People, program, service, equipment, supplies, and physical plant requirements: an asset-building plan.

PHASE III. Urgent, but deferrable objectives. $ _____

The same features but including some endowment objectives: an asset-building plan.

PHASE IV. Investment gift opportunities. $ Unlimited

Budgeted, non-budgeted and all other features desired to be endowed in perpetuity: for assets in perpetuity.

Phases I and IV are addressed to every constituent. Phase I seeks gifts from donor income to the organization's income for budget operations and from 100 percent of the individual and family constituents. Phase IV seeks a planned gift for an endowment objective from every living constituent because every living person has a Will at law.

Phase II and III are addressed to one percent to two percent of those constituents who have been rated as "appearing to being affluent" — possessors of resources of securities, property, etc., whose assets may be shared in whole or in part with the organization.

Today, the philanthropic resources an organization needs to ensure — even to insure — its mission, goals, and objectives should be all the resources it needs to thrive — not what it needs to just get by. To these ends feasibility is not a question if the organization has a thoughtful, reasonable plan, and if it has a thorough prospect research function. The question is, whether the organization's staff has the willingness and capacity to "sell" its plan to its rated constituents, not to ask its constituents to assess its unpreparedness by asking probability-of-success questions, not to ask if the organization is worth it, but to sell its worth.

This "selling" process I call "chief executive consultation conferences." Under the auspices of a trustee host, six to eight persons are called together to assess and discuss the draft case statement or prospectus with the CEO. The goal is to get ideas — positive ideas — for selling the program and to obtain a sense of ownership in the plan for a comprehensive, phased, philanthropic resource acquisition effort.

The mobilization of resources concept is a dynamic, dramatic process of confidence building among all constituents. And, this confidence building must be engineered by careful, but not protracted, administrators and governing board members to ensure the future of the organization.

Without evidence of asset-building for a certain destiny, there can be no confidence-building.

The mobilization of human resources follows the mobilization of functional services and their costs for serving society.

Asset-Building for Nonprofits

*It is no longer our resources
that limit our decisions;
It's our decisions that
limit our resources*
— *U. Thant*
*Former Secretary General
United Nations*

The term "asset-building" is usually applied to the process of increasing personal wealth. Contained therein is the hope for future comfort and unexpected financial needs. Today many of our vital nonprofit organizations have created or plan to create eight- and nine-figure capital fund programs for greater-than-ever philanthropic productivity. Capital fund programs are asset-building programs seeking diverse asset gifts for diverse purposes in an ever-changing society of involuntary forces, issues, and trends.

Given a governing board of experienced entrepreneurial leaderhip, adminstrators have the unusual opportunity to design the destiny of the organization and assess its present and future value to society. Given such a design and an assessment of value, the organization's task is to sell, sell, sell that vision and its value to insure its mission. Those organizations which do not design their destiny and sell that destiny will find soon that destiny has a design for them.

I was amazed that in 1992 — a recession year — 14 gifts from $50,000,000 to $116,000,000 were announced. Never has there been so many gifts of that size in any one year.

Too, there were 1014 gifts of $1,000,000 reported. This figure is up from 243 reported in 1983. And there are probably four to five times these figures for such gifts which were not announced.

What's happening? Organizations and institutions are assessing their values and striving for endowments of diverse features and functions which are made available to "buy." These attract constituents' interests and concerns who have the assets to share in making a difference. The traditional campaign is becoming obsolete to meet crisis after crisis. Such campaigns tell constituents that the organization has not designed its destiny including what that destiny costs. Preparing for and selling short-term and long-term fiscal stability and security builds far more confidence in management and administrative leadership than selling crisis after crisis.

Too, the availability of incredible sources for prospect research is reassuring. Individual and family philanthropic potential can be minimized by unsophisticated and unknowing trustees, officers, development personnel, and volunteers.

Some years ago, the IRS announced that we had in the United States some 300,000 individuals with annual incomes in excess of $1,000,000. A few years later, the IRS announced the figure at 400,000, and that women exceeded men in this category. Later, the IRS announced that we had 720,000 such incomes but that the increase was in people in their 30s and 40s. Who are these people in your constituency? How few do you need to make a difference in the qualitative fulfillment of your mission?

Many years ago, a distinguished public relations executive cited that there are probably 100 individuals surrounding every organization who have the capacity to affect the destiny of the organization forever. He stated further that it was the responsibility of the CEO to identify these people, cultivate their interest, and love them to death. How many of these have you identified? How many have you written off by knowledge of their present interests and failed to acquaint them with your mission, services, and goals even to changing their priorities?

The act of philanthropic giving is a voluntary decision. What rests in your hands is the art of preparation and persuasion to suggest unprecedented decisions for donor investors to make a difference.

To these ends, everyone involved in planning for an asset-building program must obtain and read the book entitled: *Achieving Excellence in Fund Raising,* by Henry Rosso (Jossey-Bass, 1981).

It is impossible to estimate the enormity of philanthropic potential available in this country. It is possible to identify the enormity of the excuses, apologies, and lack of education about why unprecedented philanthropy is not possible. These negative reasons include the absence of vision; the lack of planning; mediocre governing board membership; emphasis upon government, business and foundation resources; concentration upon paper shuffling rather than entrepreneurial salesmanship; insensitive investment counselling; and unfamiliarity with incredible planned gift instruments to benefit charities and heirs at the same time.

The Wealthy and Wise

In the November 29, 1994, issue of *The Chronicle of Philanthropy,* Claude Rosenberg, Jr., senior principal of the RCM Capital Management firm in San Francisco, California, reported from his new book, *Wealthy and Wise: How You and America Can Get the Most Out of Your Giving* (Little, Brown, 1994)*.

The title of his article is "How Philanthropy Could be $100 Billion Bigger!"

Excerpts from his article follow:

Philanthropy is missing out on at least $100 billion a year.

That is a conservative estimate of how much untapped money is available for charitable giving — dollars that are desperately needed to help solve violence, homelessness, crime, drugs, poor schools, and other problems facing the nation. How can nonprofit groups get that money and how can society insure that it will be put togood use? The answer lies in redefining and reinventing the way both donors and nonprofit organizations operate.

While the generosity of Americans far exceeds that of people in other countries, we have not even come close to our potential. Worse, in recent years, as society's needs have grown and government has become less and less able to help, philanthropy has been in decline.

---

* From *Wealthy and Wise* by Claude Rosenberg, Jr. Copyright © 1994 by Claude Rosenberg, Jr. By permission of Little, Brown and Company.

From 1980 to 1991, people with incomes that exceed $1 million saw an 80 percent rise in their incomes — and that is after adjusting for inflation. Yet their average charitable contribution declined by 57 percent.

My guess is that people are not simply selfish. Personal distractions, exaggerated financial fears, procrastination, and complex issues — such as tax laws and lack of confidence that their money makes a difference — combine to interfere with the best of intentions.

But a big reason many contributions have been lost is that donors, financial planners, and others often define surplus funds in a way that is incomplete and even naive. By and large, most contributors myopically base their giving potential on income alone, and often that figure is understated. Amazingly enough, most donors exclude their earning assets, such as: savings accounts, money-market funds, bonds, common stocks, real estate, and businesses (which often have dollar values that dwarf their owners' incomes.) In fact, people should evaluate both their incomes and earning assets — their net worth — to determine how much money they can afford to give.

The benefits of persuading people to think differently about charitable giving could be enormous. Based on my estimates of 1991 asset ownership, the average person who earned more than $1.8 million and contributed an average of $87,000 could donate approximately 10 times that or $900,000. At the same time, that person could still see growth in his or her asset wealth, which, on average, would be about $16 million in inflation-adjusted dollars. If the 50,000 to 60,000 people who have that much in income and assets were to donate such easily affordable amounts, an additional $40 billion per year could be raised. Furthermore, even with less dramatic giving increases, Americans who make $75,000 or more could comfortably contribute $60 billion more per year and see their investments grow.

While plenty of surplus capital can be made available to charities, money alone is not enough. We need stronger leadership on the part of charities and contributors alike. Now more than ever, nonprofit organizations need to consolidate, set realistic goals, and show quantifiable results.

Currently, much of our charitable giving is analogous to applying Band-Aids. It does not get at the larger, overriding problems that hamper real progress. Often self-serving special-interest groups get in the way of reform, as does burdensome government red tape. The problem is that too few nonprofit groups are in a strong enough position to remove such obstacles. And, too often, it is difficult to find legislators or politicians who will help fight for significant change. The result? Too many maladies persist, forcing contributors to turn elsewhere or give up on philanthropy in general.

Giving wisely requires thought. People who want to contribute either money or time — or both — should think about the following issues:

— What causes are of most interest to the donor? Are those areas in serious need of help? If the honest answer is *no,* isn't it better to put aside personal interests and look for a cause that will truly benefit from the donor's money and time?
— Which charity would benefit most from a donor's involvement? For example, wouldn't it be better to make a big gift to a charity that has proved its effectiveness than to scatter a dozen small donations to organizations that are experimenting with a wide range of solutions to a problem?
— Isn't it wiser to earmark gifts for charitable programs that are fighting problems today — instead of putting the bulk of contributions into endowments that will allocate only a small portion of money for current use?
— What tough questions has a donor asked about the charities he or she wants to support? Donors need to talk to organizations about their past, present, and future goals, the obstacles they face in carrying out their missions, their financial positions, and the quantifiable results they have achieved.

— Has the donor taken steps to monitor regularly the charities he or she supports to insure that contributions are being used efficiently and effectively?

Our society is crying for change, and our future is in doubt unless we alter our attitudes. Those who can best afford to make a difference should realize that as we continue to allow our massive social problems to fester, governments will choose to tax away more and more of our incomes. Those tax receipts will inevitably fall into inefficient government hands. The better approach is to pump more money into the charity world so that private organizations will have the resources they need to solve our nation's many problems. If donors start viewing their contributions as investments for our present and our future, we can put America on the road to recovery. And do not be fooled. The dollars are there for such investments.

Introducing the "Forward Fund"

The operating budget of almost every nonprofit organization contains an income gap — the budget-balancing gap — the amount of which becomes the annual fund goal to be sought from diverse private sector constituencies. This calculated gap represents very serious consideration of probable income necessary to sustain expected services of the organization. Therefore, a persistent anxiety must exist to achieve the income gap goal through extreme efforts just to assure what is — not what ought to be — in the current operating budget.

This anxiety is converted to a near crisis for the organization if the budgeted annual fund goal is not met. That anxiety is converted to both positive and negative pleas of persuasions. Those consequences, however, fall upon the organization's board of governance members and administrators alike for failure to assure both balanced budgets and enhanced services.

What follows here may contain solutions to increase both confidence in organizational management and program marketing features to inspire continuous voluntary constituency response.

First, consider obtaining and maintaining a sum of money to be used as a **forward fund.** This money is similar to profit-centered organization's venture funds.

Second, consider inviting constituents' annual investments in the organization on the basis that annual fund commitment represents income on a permanent endowment fund in their name, as if that endowment were providing interest at, say, eight percent or 10 percent in perpetuity.

Third, consider marketing the annual fund under a significant name the way capital fund/asset building programs are marketed and achieved.

These features are described as follows:

Create a forward fund. A forward fund is an amount of cash provided "up front" at the beginning of the organization's fiscal year, which can be drawn upon up to a certain point for current cash flow and which serves as a revolving fund so long as it is replenished continuously. The elements of a forward fund include:

1. securing from the least number of donors (but more than one) an amount of cash which equals the amount of the budget gap represented by the concurrent annual fund goal;

2. at the same time and from the same donors, request at least 25 percent more to serve future annual fund goals;

   Example. The annual fund goal of ABC organization is $200,000. Request $250,000 in cash from one, two, or three donors, preferably anonymously, with such funds to be applied to the current fund goal, so that requests for current fund operations will be for next year's budget. The amount over $200,000 will function with interest to cover next year's budgeted goal increase — and so on.

3. invest the amount received at the highest possible interest rate with the right to "draw down" on that amount as needed for current expenses, thus eliminating the necessity for "on line" loans at high interest rates;

4. apply income from the current annual giving program immediately as replacement for drawn down amounts;
5. replace interest from the forward fund account to the corpus of the fund assiduously;
6. monitor "draw downs" only for current cash flow, never, never for contingencies or unexpected cash requirements;
7. announce the forward fund as a new management strategy:
   a. to assure constituents that the current budget will be balanced;
   b. that budget expense crises have been replaced with an assured revolving fund; and
   c. that crisis fund raising has been replaced by investment gift requests based upon confidence in the management of the organization's fiscal affairs.

The forward fund is neither a challenge nor a matching fund. It is a basic revolving assurance fund for motivating constituents to be more generous through their investments to the organization's future. The forward fund's efficacy can be perpetual if managed with very great care — even in the event of unforeseen emergencies.

We accept the marketing fact that special capital fund programs must have significant names connoting their importance and urgency, even though they may be only of 18 months' or five years' duration.

Why should the annual fund program be less distinctive, less important, less motivating when its massive and generous basic support is so urgent and continuing?

Summary. In a society where our percentage of participation among constituents of record is so low, and where the costs of obtaining gifts is increasing too rapidly, we must give greater attention to marketing our basic programs through sophisticated nomenclature. This marketing must not be superficial; it must be born of communicating confidence, pride, and gratitude, not crises, not fear of failure.

The bottom line is philanthropy — every not-for-profit organization is a philanthropy. Each exists for the "love of humankind" — not as the result of some political edict. We should talk about philanthropy as a voluntary sharing of the resources we hold only in trust while we are here — resources for others when we are not here. Let's stop selling fund raising. Let's sell investments in our philanthropies as philanthropists like the biblical widow who gave all she had in the world.

Endowment: What Is It? How Does It Work?

Today more and more charitable organizations seek endowments, but the word is seldom explained. What is endowment, an endowment fund, and how do they work?

Endowment is the act of providing financial or other asset resources to serve as investment funds — savings accounts — the income from which, in whole or in part, may be applied to current budgeted operations, therefore providing fiscal security and stability for operations in perpetuity.

Each donor of an endowment fund, whatever its size, is an investor in helping to ensure — even to insure — the mission of the organization in meeting human needs. The corpus of such a fund remains the basic investment; only its income is used for current financial needs, or all or part of the income is returned to the corpus to increase future income.

Endowment fund income also provides a reserve income for the governing board to meet unexpected, unbudgeted needs arising from today's complex involuntary forces, issues, and trends.

Each endowment fund is unique and reflects each investor's interests, concerns, gratitude, pride, and confidence in the future of the organization.

Endowment funds can be provided for by adding a codicil amendment (a special addendum) to a personal or state will. All estate gift provisions are deductible before the assessment of federal estate tax provisions. Cash, securities, life insurance no longer needed, new life insurance, real property, and various deferred gift instruments can be acceptable to create endowment funds.

Investors may name such endowment funds as tribute, memorial or personal and family remembrances.

Every charitable organization prefers unrestricted or undesignated funds, the income from which can be used by the governing board where needed most. Preferred use and restricted gift provisions should be cleared in advance of such designations through policies of the appropriate governing board.

Endowment: These are the funds which will make possible the future of every deserving charitable organization serving our personal, spiritual, community, national and international humanitarian needs.

Ensuring Our Values with Endowments

Today we are witnessing on every nonprofit horizon earnest, even aggressive, philanthropic promotions for endowment funds from diverse personal resources for diverse human service purposes. Until rather recently, professional counsellors and administrators alike preached and taught that motivations and solicitations for endowment purposes could not be sought even from caring constituents. It was not until the last 15 to 20 years that nonprofits changed from a "new building" and a "checkbook" mentality to designed consciousness for fiscal stability and security. The means for this most desirable goal is the previously forsaken, even forbidden, endowment program.

1. Plan for endowment. Every organization must have a plan — a design — for its future. That plan must include: a) provisions for present, continuous, and increasing current budget support by all constituents including requests for assurance of receipt of the annual fund amount by bequest endowment at least; b) short-term program and service needs (capital and asset funds) which are not budgeted and will be sought from the current assets of one to five percent of the constituents in addition to their current income fund gift; and c) a list of investment gift opportunities, which are never totalled, but feature budgeted items which can be *endowed out of the budget,* and which include features not budgeted such as building and campus maintenance, acquiring updated equipment, library acquisitions, and unrestricted endowment. These features should be cited as costing from $5,000 up to seven or eight figures.

Thus, such a comprehensive resource development plan itself is a confidence builder. Every constituent can see in the plan that the organization has a design for its destiny under auspices of good management and good administration. This plan must be announced and marketed widely to stimulate even unexpected results from unknown "friends."

2. The case for endowment. Endowment must be defined, described, and evaluated as a means and motivation to ensure both personal and organizational values, interests, and concerns for perpetual impact. Many business and foundation executives are anti-endowment because they see costs of services and concurrent gifts and grants as sufficient tests of management and administrative confidence. Yet, they themselves are endowed by stockholders and corpus amounts.

Endowment funds are savings accounts and living insurance amounts. Generous endowments inspire more generous endowments.

3. Governance. Constituents contemplating the provision of endowment resources look carefully at *who* is the governing board of the organization. The *who* communicates authentication of management competence.

4. Gift and grant policies. Every organization must have a series of gifts and grants policies which are carefully reviewed annually by the entire board of trustees. These policies cite those gifts and grants which will be considered and accepted by the board of trustees including offers of gifts-in-kind. Changing Internal Revenue Service rules, regulations, and other legislation must be studied constantly for the benefit of prospective donors' anticipated offers, amounts, and conditions of recognition.

5. Planned gift policies. Every organization must have considered and approved planned gift policies considering those deferred gift devices which will and will not be acceptable and conditions that pertain to them. Some of these can be very complicated to manage and may adversely affect general organizational income.

6. Investment policies. The organization must be able and willing to communicate its board-approved investment policies to potential endowment investors. Such policies must be considered, studied, and approved by the entire board of trustees, not just its finance or executive committees. Such policies must be reviewed frequently in response to dramatically changing economic conditions.

7. Investment counsel. Today investment counsellors in our nonprofit organizations are careful analysts of just who gives endowments. Incredible investment income results are being produced by experienced, full-time investment counsellors. The corner banker is no longer viewed in the same manner as specialized investment counsellors.

8. Endowment reports. The existence, nature, source, and utilization of endowment resources should be announced at least annually in addition to any normal audit report.

9. Publications. The fact and function of endowment today is so crucial and important to the future of every organization that there should be a simple **prospectus for endowment.** This basic document is necessary before the diverse planned gift pamphlets are distributed. Further, this document should be sent to every constituent for personal, family or friend advocacy use, not just to those over age 55.

Any organization truly serious about earning deserved endowment resources must prepare for evidence of confidence in management preconditions to attract attention, inspire, motivate, and conclude unprecedented endowed investment commitments.

Kinds of Endowments

Every board member and administrator desires and prefers unrestricted, undesignated, unlimited endowment income for use when, where, and as needed. Such gifts will not happen often unless there is absolute, total confidence in the governing board and those provisions cited above.

First, it must be stated that nearly every person in the United States has a will — a will provided by state law. That law takes care of families, but not charities. Therefore, all promotions to all constituents must cite this fact as a given. Promotions should emphasize codicil amendments as easily drawn, inexpensive, appropriate documents which will stand up in any probate court, even when applied to state inheritance provisions. Further, it must be stated over and over again that estate provisions are deducted *first* before the computation of federal estate taxes.

Unrestricted endowments. The provision of resources without restraints of any kind connote absolute confidence in the management leadership of the organization and its mission, goals, objectives, and record of service to humankind. The income from such funds can be applied to present budget requirements, features needed but not budgeted, or all or part of the income returned to the corpus for additional future impact.

Preferred use endowments. Most endowment investors cite that income from their endowment resources are *preferred* to be used for features of their interest or concern unless the governing board has greater need for such income elsewhere. Too often volunteers and administrators consider these preferences as absolute restrictions, say so, record so, and thereby inhibit or limit the use of the fund income on a more flexible basis. Therefore, a *preferred use* provision is almost unrestricted in impact when negotiated as such.

Restricted endowments. Such endowment provisions must *never* be accepted by the board of trustees until and unless there is a written provision which says:

> should the provisions for use of the income from this endowment cease to exist, the board of trustees is authorized to use such income nearest to the intent of such provisions.

Many, many millions of dollars of endowed funds are "tied up" legally because of restrictive provisions. Yet, there can be no doubt that many providers of such funds never intended absolute, legal, constrictive use of such funds forever, but rather cited a preferred use. Many restrictions have, do, and may become obsolete.

To decline unacceptable restrictions is a tremendous mark of confidence to others that the organization stands on its policies and principles of management.

Living endowment. There are at least two advantages to the living endowment idea.

First, an investor can create an endowment fund in name and in fact but to be fully funded definitely at some future date, *but* the income from that endowment is provided by the donor yearly. Here the donor can *see* the endowment working while living and enjoying applied and future philanthropy.

Second, the fact that every endowment is a living, working vehicle is a very positive inspiration and motivation for others to provide likewise.

Uses of Endowment

The general understanding of endowment is that such funds and resources are forever. About 98 percent of such endowment provisions are perpetual unless excepted otherwise.

Term endowment. A donor may provide funds, resources or gift instruments which may be expended after a stated perod of time or upon the occurrence of a certain event. Such an endowment provision may underwrite costs of an anniversary celebration, of a new department or program, etc., until the event is concluded or self-supporting.

Quasi-endowment. Such an endowment provision allows the board of trustees to use such funds, including the corpus, as needed without intended perpetuity. This endowment serves as a flexible reserve for use as needed. Yet, it is still reportable as an endowment.

The forward fund. This fund serves as a quasi-endowment fund to eliminate the fiscal year-end harassment of all constituents to help assure a balanced budget. The current fund total goal can be projected over five or more years and provided by one, two or three donor investors. This fund serves as a reserve from which the business officer can draw down amounts when and as needed, where all current fund income is applied to the corpus upon receipt, and where the corpus is invested for increase in the corpus amount. Such a revealing forward fund eliminates short-term bank loans but more so enhances the sophistication of managing the current fund program.

Returned income. A great many boards of trustees have initiated policies wherein some portion of the annual income from endowment is returned to the corpus as a self-investment procedure. One organization with a 26 percent return committed 19 percent to be returned to the corpus. The endowment was small, but management was dedicated to increasing the corpus even though such action affected the usable income amount.

Recognition. Board policies must provide for basic, minimum amounts of endowed funds, which will be carried in audited statements forever under a donor, memorial or tribute name. The costs of administration of handling small funds can be great. Usually the minimum amount for a named fund is $5,000; by the year 2000 that minimum may be $25,000. No feature should be named for less than 51 percent of the total cost of the feature. Open-end funds provide the opportunity for additional investors to give to the same fund.

Sources of Endowments

There are many sources for unprecedented philanthropy about which the organization's constituency must be educated.

First, every constituent must be inspired to provide an endowment — even endowing their annual fund gift as an infinite living vehicle for human service.

Second, every constituent must be willing to learn how to become a historic philanthropist regardless of the size of assets held.

Third, every constituent must act now to ensure that preferred interests can be provided and secured given the proclivity of Congress and the Internal Revenue Service to change regulations.

The desire must precede the fact for establishing endowments in organizations wherein lies great service to humankind.

Endowments are living testimonials that what we have on earth is on loan for us to provide for others as others have provided for us.

We endow our *valuables* through insurance; isn't it time we endowed our *values* now and forever?

Let's discuss a philanthropic life wish — seeing an endowment fund working while the donor is here to see it work. Too often, endowments are provided as a death wish — created but never seen in action by the provider.

A functional endowment provides income currently for budgeted purposes or preferred uses by the provider. Countless opportunities exist in every nonprofit organization for interested, concerned, capable constituents to *ensure* — even to *insure* — a staff person, a program, a service, a facility, equipment or maintenance today and forever.

Persons with dedicated philanthropic intent can provide for an eventual endowment corpus for a preferred budgeted use as that use will cost five years from now. That endowment amount must be set aside with irreversible assurance to become fully functional in possession of the organization some day.

Effective upon written and witnessed details, the donor provides annually the amount of interest return to the organization as a tax-deductible gift. Here the provider has made a difference in meeting both today's need and tomorrow's.

Fortunately for the donor, the return the donor receives will far exceed the organization's return when the endowment corpus flows to the organization whose funds are handled by banking institutions.

Therefore, functional endowment income from and through the donor can have far greater impact now and while the philanthropist lives to see it working for humankind.

Philanthropy today must be insured for tomorrow. Functional endowment is the first step to insure for others what others have assured for us.

Capital Funds: Campaign or Fund?

The Capital Campaign. This is usually an all-out, total constituency, person-to-person solicitation for a series of specific objectives within a given timeframe with pledges or statements of intent payable over three to five years.

1. *Pro Considerations.* Such a campaign is excellent public relations or sales programs to renew or to

revitalize constituents of an organization and remind them of their importance to it. A campaign can create new donors and increase commitments of regular donors. It indoctrinates many, many volunteers to become new or renewed advocates for the organization at the grass-roots level.

2. *Con Considerations.* Such campaigns depend upon *financial* success from less than 10 percent of the constituency; but 90 percent of the effort and related expenses are public relations and are related to low productive potential. Costs for such low potential programs today are exorbitant. The enlistment of volunteers for such mass communications is increasingly difficult. Such campaigns seriously and adversely affect annual gift income where established habits of giving are important. Too, not all of the top 10 percent of the constituents are prepared to make significant commitments during the period of the campaign.

The tendency to accelerate success by the campaign method fosters a mechanical approach, pressure, and premature decisions rather than persistent, sophisticated, careful strategy dealing prospect by prospect. Tactics at the expense of strategy, resulting from impatience, can be counterproductive to the long-term benefit of the organization. Yet, no doubt, many prospects can be identified who are emotionally and financially prepared to make commitments if asked for the right (studied) gift objective, by the right persons, for the right reasons, at the right time, under the right conditions.

The Capital Fund Program. This method was born out of comprehensive analyses of the campaign method. Since some 10 percent of the constituency may be assumed to possess some capital assets, it is reasonable to address gift opportunities to them on a consistent basis while maintaining and increasing the strengths of the annual gift and deferred (planned) gift program. As with the campaign goals, gift opportunities can be set and achieved.

1. *Pro Considerations.* When created and integrated as the major gift effort of the development function, all staff and volunteers are aware that selected prospects are objects of a special program and support that effort fully. Assuming an orderly presentation of capital fund policies, procedures, priority needs, case and motivation, plus prospect tender loving care, the presentation of needs to cultivate prospects can result in continual substantial asset gift commitments. Properly staffed and implemented, the *capital fund program,* in fact, capitalizes in a financial and donor fulfillment sense, all other development and organization relations and fund programs. Too, capital fund programs are far, far less costly while being just as productive.
2. *Con Considerations.* Capital fund programs, contrary to campaigns, possess relatively lower visibility in terms of dramatically active activity. By their very nature, capital fund programs are low key, highly sophisticated, strategic programs which proceed prospect by prospect, rather than area by area, en masse, as in the campaign technique.

By its very nature, the capital fund program requires a staff officer and a key volunteer committee, each and all possessing a great sensitivity and judgmental capacity to "read" personal nuances for both cultivation and solicitation strategy determinations.

Organizations which have not provided for the systematic identification and cultivation of their potential high gift level prospects are limiting the short-term and most certainly the long-term potential of their organization. Priority capital needs and gift opportunities for endowment should be set in a program and a plan of action scheduled tightly with a "sense of campaign" — urgency and necessity to ensure, even to insure, academic, health, spiritual, service stability, and security.

Campaigns alone will not assure that security. Sophisticated management of resource programming will.

Governing boards, officers, and staff members of non-profit organizations confronting the need for substantial additional financial resources historically look to "capital campaigns." When such campaigns are successful, seldom are statistics audited objectively to determine just exactly how such programs achieved success: who gave, what amounts were given, what amounts of cash or other resources were to be committed and transferred over what periods, how much of the commitments were tied into long-term estate plans, what amount of long unreported but received bequests were counted as "current campaign income," what unrelated grants were counted, were any substantial commitments really unsubstantiated, how many prospects were never contacted? Seldom are business officers gratified with the results of "successful" campaigns because they do see the campaign statistics relating them to announced goals and urgent needs.

When campaigns are successful, commitments verified, and assets transferred, such success is achieved because a very few resources ensure that success — usually from one percent to five percent of a given constituency. Why not, then, concentrate at the outset to identify, research, study, involve, and set a strategy for each prospect to inculcate a deep desire for the prospect to achieve the greatest possible philanthropic commitment when they are ready, not just when the organization demands participation because of a campaign?

Cost benefit analyses of "successful" campaigns alone should drive governing boards and officers to seek alternate solutions to the campaign. But campaigns that only provide a temporary alternative to years of neglect of adequate resource development budgets, staff, and leadership commitments and inclination to concentrate on large gift prospects will not help matters, either.

A university merged its "annual fund" into its first capital campaign. Regular annual donors/members were not contacted for three years waiting for the gift-range table to get down to their level. When they were contacted they gave their annual gift. After the three-year gift shortfall, it took seven years to get donor/members results up to their previous high level. Hence, the "habit" of current fund results is a real phenomenon.

The ongoing, consistent, sensitive, high-gift level, sophisticated capital fund program, as opposed to the campaign, does not have the public drama of an advertising campaign. The capital fund program just goes on quietly, but consistently, adding to endowment and other needs without ballyhoo and at a very low cost. Its progress is counted in numbers of dollars, not numbers of donors.

The following distinctions between **capital campaigns** and **capital fund programs** may be helpful for governing boards and officers to more wisely decide between the true productivity of the two principal options.

Capital fund programs refer to the transference of donor assets to the assets of an organization. It is well to begin an explanation of the differentiation, with a definition (from Webster's Seventh New Collegiate Dictionary):

a. **capital,** used as a noun: a stock of accumulated goods especially at a specified time and in contrast to income received during a specified period; the value of these accumulated goods; accumulated goods devoted to the production of other goods; net worth;

b. **capital account,** used as a noun: an account representing ownership in a business; a corporation account classified as part of net worth; a capital assets account;

c. **capital assets,** used as a plural noun: long-term assets either tangible or intangible; and

d. **capital expenditure,** used as a noun: an expenditure for long-term additions or betterments chargeable to a capital assets account.

Therefore, the capital fund program of a gift-receiving agency seeks commitments of assets from the total resources of individuals *in addition to* continual annual gift support from income. Capital gifts, gifts from assets, are usually tied into an estate planning device.

Businesses and foundations may make commitments to capital fund programs over a period of time from either income or other available resources.

Capital funds — assets funds — given to an organization are usually endowment funds for people, program, operations, or plant needs. Physical plant needs are commonly referred to as capital needs since they add to the assets of the organization as a physical asset.

Annual funds, gifts from donors to organizational income, are used for budgeted or operational needs.

There is no magic in having campaigns and no magic solutions in campaigns as such. There is magic in the strategic planning for constant low-key, high-level gift programs for the production of substantial new resources. The difference rests in executive decisions based upon rational analyses of marketing the organization's financial requirements among those who make the difference in the final analysis.

Feasibility Studies — Pros and Cons

We are well into the era of surveys, market tests, polls, consumer analyses, and financial support feasibility studies. Products, services, and attitudes are constantly being tested and analyzed eventually to persuade others to buy, to use, to share, or to give an opinion. Some claim these procedures are scientific tests. At best they are "guestimates," regardless of self-serving professions to the contrary. Eventually people must buy the product or the service or change present attitudes. This is the *real* test. *Probability does not always predict reality.*

Philanthropic giving is perhaps the most intangible attitude to test next to religious beliefs or prejudices. The real test of philanthropy is the signature on a check, a securities certificate, a gift transmittal form, a statement of intent, a commitment letter, a will or estate plan or a deed of transfer of property. Verbal promises of commitment are as intangible as attitudinal analyses. Our cemeteries are full of people who promised resources to heirs and to charities which never materialized.

Fund-raising feasibility studies are similarly intangible. At best they reflect attitudes and impressions *of the moment* which can change very, very quickly — even the next moment. Such studies can answer "why not" or "if you do, what constraints you can expect," but they are unable to assess or prove realistic potential. As a prospect cultivation medium it is a failure.

Most feasibility studies are implemented by experienced fund-raising professionals as well as semi-professionals untrained in the art of direct or implied interrogation or persuasive interrogation. Too, many studies are implemented when the professional is unfamiliar with the breadth and depth of the personality of the client or of the respondent or with the options of concrete market-testing devices.

Perhaps 90 percent of such studies are conducted when the organization is far, far from ready to implement the expected program. Thus the "test" is premature and creates an attitude of expectancy on the part of the respondent which, if the program does not soon mature, can be crucially counterproductive, which adversely affects those respondents. Unfortunately, professionals press for immediate feasibility studies as a "foot in the client door," for sequential retention and/or for the productive utilization of unassigned personnel. Yet, the feasibility study is a useful device when properly timed, adequately prepared for and conducted by a trained interviewer.

The urgency and necessity for increased financial support is an understandable reason for testing the probability of desired gift/grant productivity, whether for increased budget support, asset-building capital fund programs, and/or endowment funds. However, such urgency should not dominate reason through naive or gullible actions that may *prematurely alert or alarm* potential donors or volunteer leaders. Thoughtful administrators can retain reputable, experienced professional counsellors to assess *internal* management, administrative and staff preconditions and preparedness before any attempt is made to "test" probabilities with any *external* constituent or constituency. An experienced professional who has been through the fires of disappointment and the glows of success can ascertain in two or three days' time conditions necessary for increased private sector philanthropic productivity. Such a preliminary audit — a state of readiness analysis — can be invaluable to administrators and to trustees. Too, such an audit can prevent embarrassing verbal and written reports of problems and constraints which can and do undermine trustee/volunteer confidence in administrative competence. When accomplished and heeded, the audit can accelerate the organization's preparedness to initiate a *properly timed* external audit, and capitalize upon its strengths and minimize weaknesses.

Given these vagaries of procedure, timing, and results, what are the preliminary requirements for a truly productive philanthropic resource development audit and how can results be honestly, objectively evaluated? Then, with all this erudition, are so-called feasibility studies really necessary? Discussion of these points follow.

Preliminary requirements. If a feasibility study is to result in an adequate test of philanthropic potential and that test be followed by a systematic, progressive plan of action, then the organization:

1. must have a studied plan for, say, at least five years anticipating services and programs to be budgeted and/or funded;
2. must have a financial plan of costs and contingencies for the approved plans and programs;
3. must have represented on its board the kind of leadership who can serve as authenticators and leaders not only in advocacy but also in personal gift commitments;
4. must have a sales-oriented, production-oriented, creative development staff;
5. must have a comprehensive financial development program for annual support, capital fund and planned gift policies and opportunities; merchandising — putting ideas on the shelf for people to buy; and to endow budget relief items;
6. must have identified, researched, and cultivated prospects *capable* of providing the kind and level of gift support expected, estimating capacity not proclivity; and
7. must have a motivational sales case or prospectus for substantial philanthropic support meager on history,

dynamic on services, and competent on projections for the future.

Too, with a majority of respondents, lists of proposed prospects can be rated and analyzed for crucial personal evaluations on a confidential basis to add further substance to a dull, routine attitudinal analysis. (Of course, the respondent's name would be excluded from such a listing.)

The study interviewer and analyst must be adept in guiding each interview to achieve preplanned results of involvement and constructive responses. Further, the interviewer must offer to leave at the appointed time — 45 minutes to one hour. Should the respondent request the interviewer to stay, so be it. The interviewer is then on the respondent's time. But the time must be judiciously used. No gossip. No rumor test. No feeder complaint questions. If such problems exist, they will come out in a relaxed constructive atmosphere.

The entire interview process is a cultivation, a sales process; even if the respondent is thoroughly on the side of the organization, its leadership, its services, and its programs.

The interviewer must never be in the position of acting as a prosecuting attorney or junior high school yearbook advertising salesperson. The desirable stakes are too high.

Throughout the interview process, the interviewer must watch for body language, facial expressions, conflicting verbal statements, comparative illustrations, tonal inflections of conversation, and other personal traits which must be carefully weighed in accurate reports of statements, impressions, and implied attitudes. No interview is ever a mere "yes" or "no" exercise. Cultivation study process is an art in preparation, an art in implementation, and an art in analysis of the entire interview environment.

Evaluation. Each client is at the mercy of the interviewer in terms of analyzing and reporting honestly each interview and the composite of all interviews. The integrity of the interviewer is at stake from the beginning of the exercise but even more so in the preparation of analyses and recommendations. It goes without saying that nearly 100 percent of those who conduct so-called feasibility studies intend to offer a constructive service for the organization and for themselves. Yet, many such persons may be subject to personal pressures themselves. For instance, many interviewers do not debrief themselves immediately after each interview to record each detail while it is fresh. Many persons will conduct four or five interviews in a day and write reports up at the end of the day trying to remember intimate nuances and vital statements and impressions. Some persons will interview 10, 20, 30, 50 or more respondents then write up reports. The reader can use the three examples cited to assess the validity of an ultimate recommendation. And there may be other personal pressures which can affect reports and recommendations.

Evaluations which are finalized at a firm's home offices often predetermine report results and recommendations and some scarcely resemble the client status. Boilerplate is sold over and over and over. Corporate positions and pressures, too, can dominate recommendations for local situations. Professional writers usually sterilize vital personal, intimate, indigenous, relevant information, and data with journalistic jargon-ese even in the most ideal interview reports.

Organizations should insist upon a personal, on-site, immediate, *exit debriefing* of the interviewer before he or she returns to the home office or personal office for immediate impressions before they are "laundered" in a formal and sometimes formidable report document.

State of readiness audit evaluations reflect the experience, the personality, the prejudices and the impressions of the interviewer. Feedback from respondents to the chief executive of the organization is vital *before* receipt of the official report. A test of the generic efficacy of the test process is certainly appropriate.

The evaluation is a difficult process for any interviewer who realizes its vital importance to the organization. The organization should expect an honest, objective analysis; expect criticism; expect doubts about future potential; expect concerns about leadership, etc.; and expect constructive reports. An honest report will not "whitewash" interviews or respondents' statements, always maintaining absolute confidentiality, of course.

Hence, the receptivity of an honest feasibility report requires the same regimen of integrity on the part of the organization as that which is expected of the study interviewer or the firm.

Is this trip necessary? If the conditions necessary cited above are in place and poised to perform, a cultivation study by whatever name is absolutely unnecessary.

If the planning process was thorough, involving really key governing board leadership;

If the composition of the governing board has been designed and fulfilled with balanced influence as well as affluence and access among its members;

If the prospect research procedure has identified and thoroughly, repeat thoroughly, provided comprehensive documentation on the top 50, 75 or 100 prospects;

If the governing board and key constituents are confident of the competence of administrative and resource development leadership;

If the development program and process is thorough, comprehensive and progressive;

If the proposed program(s) intended to be subjected to a feasibility study can be timed and phased on a progressive basis; and

If the case for substantial and continuing support is very well put together, highly motivational and realistic — then,

A feasibility study of potential is not needed.

What is needed is a plan of action prepared by experienced and competent persons to analyze all of the above and to create an operational plan. Given all of the above, a feasibility study can be the cause for undermining the credibility of all elements of the preparation. Immediately, feasibility study proponents will scream that such a study validates and advances the elements cited. Perhaps so, but at what unnecessary expense of dollars and time? If all the basic elements are in place and in abundance and if confidence in administrative leadership exists in abundance, then set a plan of action and get on with the job in full faith and confidence that the planning processes have been thorough, are credible, and represent realistic goals for needed services, stability, and security.

Philanthropic program success must be designed and earned from the inside out. When the conditions necessary are well designed, when deserved support is earned, philanthropy will be generous. Philanthropists and philanthropoids eagerly look for confidence and competence in the organization's design for its own destiny. They are not impressed by feasibility studies!

Today the amount of money and resources an organization seeks is first a public declaration of its estimate of its worth to society, not what it needs to get by. That philanthropic resource declaration serves as a crucial motivation for affluent individuals and families to determine their part of that total they wish to commit from their resources to the organization's assurance of quality and fiscal stability and security.

Remember: Money is the root of all excellence. Never planned for. Never sought. Never received. Never used for the benefit of humankind.

Prospect Research, Persuasive Cultivation, and Results

Major philanthropic gifts and grants don't just happen. They must be designed to happen by the requesting organization.

Before prospect cultivation can result in philanthropic productivity, the organization must be ready for large gift commitments, whether for operations, special projects or programs, physical plant, endowment or all of these.

Management Preconditions: Large gift prospects look for evidence of features of confidence-building before investing generously in the mission, goals, objectives, and services or perpetuity of an organization.

First, they look to see *who* are members of the governing board. They look for evidence of competence and experience of board members who are ultimately responsible for the wise management of the organization through studied policies, procedures, and evaluations.

Second, they look for who the chief officers are in terms of their personal and professional qualifications and characteristics to administer board policies and procedures to ensure the mission, goals, services, and funding of the organization.

Third, they look for evidence of services rendered as incentives to ensure continuity. Prospects need quantifying data on the validity of professed performance in human services.

Fourth, they look for evidence of long-range planning — the design for the future or destiny of the organization given society's dynamic changes.

Fifth, they look for evidence of effective and efficient management of human and other resources, balanced budgets, the absence of debt, and acceptable returns on present endowment resources.

When an organization seeks large gifts; that is, gifts of over $1,000, the major question and posssible limiting factor is whether the organization is fundable. Has it been in existence long enough to warrant truly large gifts, gifts of $100,000 and up? Has it created current fund gift club programs in excess of $1,000 annually — $5,000; $10,000; $25,000; $50,000; and $100,000 to attract and hold major gift donors for current operations? Truly large capital fund or asset-building gifts for physical plant, equipment or endowment come first from donors who are already current fund investors. Consistent, high-level gift promotion of current fund gifts builds confidence for even larger gift investments whether cash, securities or diverse planned gift instruments.

Long-term plans are sterile unless they are costed out on a sequential or phased basis of anticipated need or financial availability. Too, organizations must have a studied list of features it would be nice to have endowed.

These endowed investment gift opportunities are never totalled because they are marketing features to attract donor/ investor interests.

Each organization must have a gift and grant policy citing those gifts which are acceptable, those which are preferred, and those which are not acceptable because of Internal Revenue Service regulations or local exclusions. This policy statement would also cite those deferred gift devices which are acceptable and those which are not. Too, that statement should cite unrestricted gifts as most desired for use where needed, and then "preferred use" gifts with no *absolute* restrictions as to use. Restricted gifts must never be accepted unless the donor provides a statement that, when the cited use no longer exists, the governing board can use the income for purposes nearest to the intent of the donor.

Many large gift prospects request information, even documents, concerning investment policies, investment counsellors, and uses of investment funds.

Administrative Preconditions. One of the major limiting factors for large-gift productivity is the absence of an attitude of expectancy. Quality costs. Persons of fiscal substance know that quality costs. Organizational progressions of quality must be translated into sums and goals which connote quality to potential donors of substantial gift commitment capacity. A $100,000 endowed professorship, today, is an insult. Even $1,000,000 will not be great by the year 2000.

Chief executive officers, resource development staff, and volunteers must be "people" persons, must have an entrepreneurial zeal for building fiscal stability and security, must be artists in the art of persuasive writing and speech, and must possess the poise of visible confidence.

These persons must have a unique intuitive sense in all contacts with prospects of substantial potential. They must be creative, sensitive, caring, and — above all — good listeners.

There exists no formula, no time schedule, no guarantee as to how long it takes from the time a prospect is identified as being a truly substantial prospect to the time for asking for a major philanthropic commitment or when that commitment can be expected.

To bring a certified prospect from unawareness of the organization, or apathy about it, or concerns about it, to the point of considering an investment in it, is like bringing a vague night dream to reality. Prospect orientation or cultivation is an art of diverse communications, not just a system of impersonal mechanical operations.

Next Step — Prospect Research: Given basic, comprehensive, public information about prospects, what's next? Once initiated, the constituency research process never ends. Each staff member and each volunteer must develop a continuous alertness for the appearance of additional information about rated prospects from diverse media sources, clubs, associations, events, professional and social meetings, parties, etc.

The second screening process becomes very personal and very crucial.

Create an *ad hoc* (temporary) committee on leadership resources of five to seven well-connected persons with a governing board member to serve as chair. Members will be asked to serve one time on a confidential, no-announcement basis to assist in rating individuals and families for gifts of leadership time for various positions and for leadership gift potential in present or future asset-building programs. Bank officers should not be asked to serve publicly but may assist in their offices on a one-to-one basis.

Meetings should be scheduled at 4:00 pm, for dinner, or after dinner when persons do not have to cut short their attendance. The resource development staff officer must be present and, in fact, conduct the meeting hosted by the chair. The chief executive officer should be present also. No discussion of personal time or resources of persons present should be permitted. Sessions should not last more than two hours. Additional sessions will require totally different members. No list of "suspects" or "prospects" should be sent in advance. Flat lists of names, addresses, and relationships only should be available. The resource development officer must hold all files of research data, proceed down the list name by name, ask questions, make notes, and press for information as follows:

1. What business, church, social, civic, fraternal, health-care, or other volunteer leadership positions has or does the individual hold? His/her spouse?
2. What is known about wife/husband, family, business and charitable interests, inheritances, financial capacity, positions, etc.?
3. Does the person have volunteer leadership interests or capacity if asked? What are perceived levels of

leverage for local, regional national, professional contacts?
4. Is there potential for future volunteer leadership positions?
5. Is the person known to be generous?
6. Is he/she known to be well-disposed toward the organization? Are gripes known?
7. Who knows the person best? Can that person develop the prospect's interest best? Who could?

For Philanthropic Potential: Giving capability or potential must be determined on the basis of the individual's total assets: For *annual* giving — individual or family *annual* income; for *capital* (asset) giving — all sources of current capital assets: securities, stock options, real or personal property, current or new insurance, family foundation or trust; business firm resources; for *estate or planned giving* from total assets — past or anticipated inheritances, personal and business properties, insurance, residences, farms, resorts, ranches, leases, patent rights, royalties, copyrights, oil and mineral rights, and collections of all kinds.

8. Is the person/family a candidate for an annual current fund gift?
   a. over $50,000
   b. over $25,000
   c. over $10,000
   d. over $5,000
   e. over $1,000
   f. over $500
9. Is the person a candidate for a capital asset fund gift from assumed assets in addition to continual current fund support?
   a. $1,000,000 up
   b. $500,000 up
   c. $250,000 up
   d. $100,000 up
   e. $50,000 up
   f. $25,000 up
   g. $10,000 up

10. Is the person a candidate for a planned gift by bequest or other deferred gift instrument?
11. What is known or suspected about total family financial capacities?
12. What is known or suspected about business gift capacities?
13. Does the individual or family have a personal foundation?
14. Is there promise for large gift capacity in the near future, say 5 to 10 years?
15. Who are the person's/family's counsellors: legal, accounting, banking, real estate, religious, investment, etc.? And many more questions. . . .

Resource Coding. The following are suggested rating codes in terms of organization interest, annual gift capacity, capital (asset) gift capacity and planned gift potential:

Organizational Interest

close to organization	I 1
could be close	I 2
not close	I 3
very distant	I 4

Annual Gift

$10,000 up	A 1
5,000 up	A 2
1,000 up	A 3
500 up	A 4

Capital Gift

$1,000,000 up	C 1
100,000 up	C 2
25,000 up	C 3
10,000 up	C 4

Planned Gift

Soon	—	P 1
Perhaps	—	P 2
Later	—	P 3
Never	—	P 4

Source of Gift Potential:

P — Personal	SF — Spouse Family
F — Family	B — Business
S — Spouse	FT — Foundation or Trust
	BF — Business Friends

Volunteer Leadership Potential:
T   — Trustee, regent, overseer, or. . . .
H   — Honorary trustee, honorary degree, or other
       honorary position
AD   — Academic, health, program council
Dev — Development — public relations and/or fund-
       raising committees
An   — Annual fund
Ca   — Capital fund
PG   — Planned gift council
N   — National leadership prestige/leverage
PO   — Parents/patients, client organization
CC   — Community committee
PR   — Special publicity, marketing, political resource
       assistance, etc.
L   — Leadership potential
AL   — Alumni/parent/grandparent leadership

The quantity of such information can come about only in the group dynamics of a few individuals; seldom can one count upon the scope of information desired on a one-on-one basis or among large groups (more than seven persons).

Productive Cultivation: Great philanthropy, in the donor's terms, results from a deep, personal sense of concern; evidence of confidence in the organization; and a strong desire to assist by being a significant party to the impact of the organization's services to humankind.

The cultivation and evaluation process can be reduced to a practical formula:

$$\frac{\text{Positioning (Plan)}}{\text{Preparation (Case)}} \times \frac{\text{Prospect}}{\text{Research}} \times \frac{\text{Presentation}}{\text{(Cultivation)}} \times$$

$$\frac{\text{Promotion}}{\text{(Involvement)}} \times \frac{\text{Perspiration}}{\text{(Persuasion)}} = \frac{\text{Productivity}}{\text{(Gifts \& Grants)}}$$

All elements leading to substantial philanthropic gifts and endowment investments are contained within this formula.

One key feature for the orientation of prospects is the chief executive consultation conference. Here small groups of individuals and/or couples are hosted by a governing board member or a prominent friend to meet the organization's chief executive officer (CEO). The CEO is the "voice" of the organization. At these occasions, the CEO has an intimate opportunity to informally explain the following attributes and concerns of the organization:

1. history and evaluation of the organization;
2. mission, goals, and objectives;
3. people, programs, and services;
4. constituents — clients, patients, members, etc.;
5. sources of financial support;
6. leadership and volunteer services;
7. plans for the future;
8. outstanding leadership and voluntary gifts;
9. impact on community needs; and
10. how people help people through the organization.

At the same time that the CEO is describing the organization, the CEO can learn from the prospect's questions, comments, facial expressions, body language, etc., about:

1. the prospect's empathy for what has been or is being said about the organization;
2. personal interests, including charitable priorities;
3. civic, business, professional, family interests, concerns and priorities;
4. missing features about the organization not covered;
5. personality and other characteristics relative to volunteer and/or governing board candidacy; and
6. friends, hobbies, children, parents, etc.

All such meetings must be of a general, get-acquainted, non-fund-raising nature but should lead to future contacts, including visits to the organization's facility.

Certified special prospects should:

1. receive general letters from the CEO about special organizational events;
2. receive newsletters stamped "ADVANCE COPY";

3. receive basic organizational documents; e.g., catalogs, newsletters, special reports of staff, etc.
4. invitations to CEO and board receptions; recognition, cultural, sport, lectures, events;
5. facility tour and contact with staff, members, students, patients, etc.

At an appropriate time, the prospect should be called upon to become a donor/investor in the current/annual fund at the highest, repeat highest, level assumed to complement the capacity and importance of the prospect's future interest in the organization. The proper person or two should make the contact as an invitation to invest in the organization's mission and goals. Following such an investment/solicitation session, there must be a thorough debriefing of every possible context of the meeting — location, nature of conversation, prospect's verbal and body language, personality traits and characteristics, as well as questions, comments, excuses or impressions about the organization.

The prospect may also be invited to consider joining a special council or committee if these groups have definite, written position descriptions, function statements, and desired personal characteristics.

The "persistence" factor contained in the formula above is implemented by the resource development officer in both intuitive and creative strategies implemented somewhat as follows:

Given 50 truly qualified top prospects:

1. something should happen to five to 10 of those persons considered to be most ready for a strong relationship and fiscal support *each week* in the name of the organization; birthday, anniversary, holiday, recognition cards; letters; invitations; copies of articles, etc.
2. something should happen to the next 10 to 25 persons determined to be "secondary" top prospects *each month* until they can be brought closer and closer to interest in the organization; and
3. something should happen to the next 25 who appear to be "tertiary" top prospects *each sixty days.*

Here is where the attributes of tender loving care, patience, and persistence are vital without the slightest appearance of aggressive behavior. *Care demonstrated will result in care returned.* Executive and staff members must be advocates of the intangibles of social/human psychology and not mere technicians of high-tech manipulation.

Negotiated Solicitation: Persons with substantial resources must be asked for gifts/investments at levels which complement their estimate of their capacity and desire to make a difference — even a difference anonymously. That request, that solicitation, in terms of the amount requested tells the prospect the value and importance of the need more than mere words can tell.

In reality, philanthropic gift solicitors are investment counsellors asking for the consideration of an investment as if that gift were the income on an endowment fund. Voluntary gifts are investments for balanced budget operations, for personnel, for investing when they do not like fund raising per se.

Let's examine again some basic principles of human behavior observed, studied, and/or assumed:

First consider the prospect —

1. People want to belong, want to be a part of the solution of a perceived need, part of a successful venture.

2. People must be convinced of the need, the logic of the program to meet the need, the confidence in the governing board and in the administrators to use funds properly, and the importance of their investment.

3. People are complimented by being asked to give at a level and at a time which complements their estimate of interest, concern, and potential impact of their leadership position to act first.

4. People who are not asked to give in accordance with their own estimates of their capacity immediately know that the asker either:
   • is not convinced of the importance of the project;
   • has not given himself/herself;

- has not done homework as to the prospect's potential or importance; or
- does not have a carefully studied financial support plan.

5. People who are the potential donors are the only ones who decide just what their gift is to be in the final analysis.

6. People who are substantial prospects for above-average gifts merit a personal call by at least one person and may be turned off from major gift participation by letters, phone calls, written proposals, and/or expensive printed publications.

7. Prospects for substantial gifts should not be visited by more than two persons except in most unusual situations.

8. Substantial gift prospects determine their participation in terms of their estimate of their part of the total fund goal.

9. People respond to goals and deadlines.

10. It is far more important to consider what happens after a solicitation which does not result in an immediate, signed commitment.

Now consider the solicitor —

11. He/she must know the program case, goals, strategy, timing, gift procedures, results, etc.

12. He/she must first be a donor.

13. He/she must know the prospect's personalilty, position, nuances, eccentricities, habits, hobbies, family, other involvements — insofar as possible.

14. Some solicitors prefer to call on friends; this can be dangerous — the friend can always say "you know that I cannot do that."

15. Some solicitors prefer to call on strangers for a more objective presentation; there is no one good answer to the strategies of #14 and #15 — people are different.

16. The solicitor is presenting
    - a need;
    - a plan;
    - a solution;
    - an opportunity for participation;
    - a method for participation monthly or annually; and
    - a successful result.
17. The solicitor must ask, repeat *must* ask, for a level of participation — a specific gift range or else the prospect does not really know what the solicitor expects of him/her. Suggest a token gift, a leadership gift, a challenge gift or to "just go along with the gang," which can be handled by letter.
18. The solicitor must not accept "no" for a final answer; leave the door open for further consideration.
19. The solicitor must never leave the gift transmittal form, statement of intent, membership card or pledge card — it is the key for the next interview.
20. The solicitor must report *every* detail of the interview conversation and describe the entire environment surrounding the prospect, all for further study of his/her interests, comforts, etc.

Asking for the investment gift commitment is an intangible sales situation. The art of conversation, establishing common ground, presenting the motivational case, suggesting participation, persuading, responding, and closing is an individual experience.

Philanthropic gift participation offers only intangible rewards of self-satisfaction; gratitude in being able to share, to help; personal fulfillment, spiritual solace; quiet pride.

Everyone, repeat everyone, who can sell confidently and enthusiastically the value, even the indispensability of his/her institution or organization, *can* ask for a gift by suggesting an investment — if the solicitor realizes that the donor innately desires to participate.

Why not, then, proceed this way:

We have discussed the program and how crucial it is that it be successful. I am sure that you know we have been busy studying the strategy for success that you would want ensured. And we have discussed your participation.

It is not my/our mission here to tell you what to do. We do want you to know that we had hoped you would consider a gift in the range of $500 to $1000 a month as your fair share as part of this program.

It just may be that you will wish to play a larger part, or consider a challenging or matching gift, or a special memorial or tribute fund. We just don't know what or how you wish to invest in our future.

Should a gift be offered which is so small as to insult the organization, the program, the objectives, and the solicitor, decline the gift graciously, as being inconsistent with the prospect's importance in the community and the organization preferring to discuss his/her leadership participation at another time.

After the interview, a debriefing session should be held to plan a resolicitation by a different approach, different solicitor, different environment. But always write thanks for each interview, whatever the outcome.

Very, very often the first gift commitment of a new prospect will not be his or her consummate gift for the organization. Rather, it will be a test — a test of the organization's management and administration, talent, and skill in the use of the funds or resources offered. It will be a test to see if the first evidence of tender loving care will be continued. So often it is not!

Summary: The prospect research function is like taking a road map out of its folder. You have the right map. Which and where are the interstates? These will make the difference in getting from here to there.

Then when the interstate is determined the analogy turns to gardening — the planting of a seed. What is the nature of the soil condition and its latent growth elements? How deep is the seed planted? How often is it watered and fertilized? When is it staked to strengthen its growth to full maturity? The first blossoms become the fruit in the annual fund. Then, comes the fruit in the full substance of its energy for asset-building, whether applied to human/personnel needs, facility, programs, endowment or all of these. After the fruit is plucked, the leaves and stalk are "cultivated" for next year's seed, growth, and fruit.

Remember: A hand not extended — in identification, in cultivation, in tender loving care, in patience — is in no position to receive.

The Case Statement as a Factor of Institutional Management and Development

Role of the Case Statement

To secure volunteer leadership or funds from whatever source, a psychological process must take place before success results. The stages of this process are *attention, interest, confidence, conviction, desire,* and *action.* The best means devised to date to compress these stages over the shortest possible time span toward action is the case statement — a concise set of persuading features and factors designed to motivate people to do something on behalf of the institution.

The case statement is one of the initial key management requirements for successful institutional development. It must be a motivational document — persuasive, not merely an essay of either glorification or need for survival. It represents a basic step — along with institutional planning, documented needs, research and evaluation of constituency, leadership enlistment, volunteer organization, staff, and budget — that must be accomplished toward winning greater philanthropic support. A case statement should be kept up to date and relevant. It should be the product of continuous planning and self-study.

Experience has shown that a sophisticated and carefully developed case together with the active involvement of prime trustees and other volunteer leadership are the two most critical elements affecting an institution's ability to receive available financial support. Without an effective statement of the case, there is less than full readiness for convincing individuals, foundations, businesses, and associations to invest in the institution's future.

Nature of the Case Statement

The case statement sets forth the arguments or the "sales features" for the institution — its mission, goals and programs, past and present accomplishments, distinctive role, services to the community, value to society, future opportunities, requirements for faculty, staff, facilities and finances, and plan of action for accomplishing future goals. It must:

1. justify and explain the status of the institution, its programs and needs so as to lead to advocacy and actual support;
2. attempt to win the reader and evolve from a description of a larger role and need to the particular destiny of the institution;
3. be positive, forward-looking, and confident with all facts and projections, reasonable, clear, vital, and accurate;
4. carefully set forth the fund-raising plans in terms of policy, priority, and endurable results. The following questions must be anticipated and answered: Why this institution? Why now? Why me? How?;
5. be so clear and concise as to accomplish its goals in a reasonable time period.

Use of the Case Statement

The case statement is most profitably used *first* as an internal document for the institutional family — administrators, faculty, constituents — to resolve, sharpen, and focus their planning and policies into a written statement that interprets its design for the future in interesting language and facts.

Second, the statement serves to create joint ownership around a prospectus, policy, plan, and sales story. It is the expression of procedures, policies, and plans agreed upon by the board of trustees and aggressively promoted by development, constituents, and other volunteer groups.

Third, the statement serves as a vital tool in "campaigning" for leadership. The enlistment of new trustees and top volunteers will be facilitated by the existence of a statement that argues the case for stability and security as well as for leadership and gift support. In addition, the ability to recruit quality staff will be enhanced by communicating the case effectively.

Fourth, it serves as a supporting tool in obtaining unprecedented annual, capital, and special gifts through tailored requests to selected prospects of considerable gift potential.

Fifth, it serves as a basic reference guide for promotional publications and communications of various kinds to the institution's public — alumni, parents, friends, religious groups, foundations, business firms, associations, and government resources.

Production of the Case Statement

The case statement described here should be printed on an attractive color paper stock. Pages should be bound in loose-leaf fashion with care given to size of type. The word DRAFT should be in red ink in the upper right corner on page one. There should be flexibility for easily and inexpensively changing pages and revising copy. Produced in this fashion, the case statement serves as a flexible management instrument for achieving a variety of objectives. Of course, each new issue must be dated.

Summary of the Case Statement

A motivational, honest case statement will transform apathy for every organization into a cause that moves people into action. When done and done properly, the case can challenge the entire organization toward greater service and enthusiastic support in fulfilling its vision, mission, founding purposes, and humanitarian results.

Managing Volunteers

These Americans are the most peculiar
people in the world. You'll not believe it when I tell
you how they behave. In a local community in
their country, a citizen may conceive of some need
which is not being met. What does he do? He
goes across the street and discusses it with his
neighbor. Then what happens? A committee begins
functioning on behalf of that need, and you won't
believe this but it is true. All of this is done by
private citizens on their own initiative.

The health of a democratic society may
be measured by the quality of functions
performed by private citizens.

— Alexis de Tocqueville (1835)

Volunteers in every nonprofit organization are people who care about their neighbors and their humanitarian needs. They become partners in planning, in producing, and in proving the indispensable value of their gifts of time, talent, personal treasure, and experience.

The productivity of volunteers, whether trustees, members of councils or other constituent groups, depends upon the credibility of their function and their ultimate success. Yet, hundreds of thousands, even millions, of dollars are spent for publications, publicity, meals, travel, and support services for the traditional purposes of public relations in the blind hope that such expenditures will result in greater and greater interest, concern, support and advocacy in their productive role.

One need only look at financial support and membership records, those which are constructed from bases of valid data, to decry the low percentages of productivity in a society of intellectual and financial affluence unprecedented in the world's history. One need only see that the nation's giving levels, while increasing perceptibly each year, are increasing at a low rate compared to increases in the gross national product. One need only look at each organization's operating budget to realize that financial support, if it increases, increases at a lower rate than necessary for salary, utility, printing, postage, and other administrative costs. One need only analyze the productivity records of volunteers themselves (not those records for which they are given credit) program by program, organization by organization, to question the validity of using volunteers in the first place. One must recognize that organizations with high financial support records are successful because of the larger and larger numbers of full-time persons employed in the productive development function. This fact recognizes that we are in a period of decreasing volunteer activity and effectiveness, all arguments to the contrary notwithstanding. All of these factors and more cite the necessity for training better administrative managers than we now have and/or the re-examination of the function as an aggressive, high-production, professionally staffed sales management effort.

Volunteer managers must ascertain in cold, calculating terms *if and when volunteers are needed,* exactly what kinds of persons are needed, exactly what they will be asked to do and exactly who will help them to perform effectively. There can be no shortcut to rigorous administrative discipline in planning nor in the implementation of programs if organizations intend to reap the support harvest which is theirs for the asking.

Planning for the effective use of a volunteer sales force is as crucial for administrative managers as planning for the programs those volunteers are to sell. Successful selling is directly proportionate to the time, care, and planning expended for the enlistment and training of the salespersons. Once the volunteers are carefully identified and studied as to potential effectiveness, carefully and honestly informed as to role, function, and urgency for productivity, then expert administrators can function to motivate, inspire, and assist volunteers to succeed early and in full measure.

Determining if volunteers are really needed is an important decision. Considering given programs in the general advancement function, one must plan and project exactly what the volunteer is expected to accomplish, in what manner, in what time frame, with what assistance — staff, materials, etc. — after having been trained or retained to ensure the expected success.

Then volunteer candidates must be carefully studied as to their qualifications and capacity to succeed if enlisted to perform a certain role and function. Mere availability does not guarantee productivity. Personal interests, concerns, nuances, eccentricities, proof of success in efforts and commitment are necessary qualities if the candidate will perform as he or she may agree to. Candidates must be matched to the function and to each other as a group — a team — a sales force.

What do volunteers expect of managers? They expect that:

1. the volunteer manager needs them to help accomplish urgent purposes for the organization;
2. the plan for their utilization will be carefully and thoroughly prepared for immediate action;
3. there will be no hidden agenda, no surprises — all facts, issues, and problems will be presented and discussed at the time of enlistment and training;
4. enlisted team members will be peer leaders who have had similar experience, responsibilities, potential, capacity, and commitment;
5. volunteer managers will train them thoroughly, effectively, interestingly, and fairly;

6. volunteer managers will not "use" or "misuse" them; and
7. they will receive continuous assistance and suggestions to help ensure success of the programs for which they are enlisted.

Do volunteers have rights once enlisted to perform certain functions? Yes, they do.
Some of their "rights" include the following:

1. the right to know all aspects of the problem or program they are expected to assist in; this includes past, present, and future analyses; anticipated deterrents or constraints;
2. the right to be treated as Very Special Persons giving of time, energy, and resources — not as non-paid part-time employees, yet not to treat as prima donnas;
3. the right to an assignment appropriate for personal attributes which would permit reasonable accomplishment;
4. the right to consistent guidance and assistance to accelerate the probability of success;
5. the right to offer advice, constructive suggestions; and
6. the right to appropriate recognition for a job well done — but none for non-performance.

Our society was built largely because people volunteered to help their neighbor in any kind of adversity. Whether such motivation was spiritual, defensive or protective does not matter. The fact is, it happened because people wanted to help. This same desire to help exists today — wanting to be needed, wanting to share, wanting to help — out of a sense of gratitude for blessings received or to help an organization succeed in its noble goals, programs, and services. Therefore, the volunteer manager must not be viewed as just another administrative clerk to get a traditional job done again this year. The volunteer manager should be a specialist, a professional manager of unlimited human resources — confident, competent, proud, productive, efficient, effective, sensitive, and with a good sense of humor — a people person.

Professionalism in Institutional Advancement

What is a professional? How does one become a professional? How is professionalism evaluated? What are the values in being recognized as a professional? Who says that you are a professional?

Our society recognizes professionalism in many areas by credentials, by testing, by evaluation, never by acclamation. We have become suspicious of academic degrees alone — credential programs and evaluation processes only cite a temporary, elusive determination of personal qualities and values, manual or intellectual skills, and accumulated personal or observed experience. We could look into history and see that the period of working apprenticeship was long, weary, and arduous before being accredited as a craftsman. There are no instant craftsmen. There are no instant professionals. Neither titles nor certificates make professionals. High, inappropriate salaries, also, do not make professionals.

It seems to me that professionalism is an earned appellation by peers who have observed evidence of direct personal accomplishment against perceived criteria, usually unstated. There are many leaders in our field of nonprofit institutional advancement who decry the term "professional" as applied to us. They refer to us as tradesmen and to our field as a trade. This is more harsh than necessary.

Then there is quite a diverse appellation applied to our field. In July 1948, Dr. Arnaud C. Marts, then president of Marts and Lundy, stated at a staff conference banquet that if we are playing a small part in making our distinctive nonprofit institutions more fiscally secure, then we are playing a part in the ministry of what our American democracy is all about. Think about this for a while.

From tradesman to minister (or ambassador with portfolio) or from apprentice to craftsman, who we are and who we become begins with our own perception of ourselves and how we decide to enhance that perception through demonstration. Each person must earn the right to be called a professional. There are people in our field who make a profession out of attending seminars, workshops, schools, courses, even to obtain fund raising degrees, who are not back home long enough to apply their "learning." There are pseudo-professionals who give lectures and give advice to those of us in our field who themselves were never in our field; yet, they tell us how to behave, how to perform, and what to do. Here we find a plethora of academic, legal, accounting, and banking "authorities," righteous in their own fields, "training" the unsuspecting in our field. Let this be a warning to all newcomers in our field: Do not attend any program, buy any book, or take to heart any article until or unless you personally check out the background of each presenter as qualified to teach you, and certainly do not waste good money chasing rainbows, however beautifully described.

An institutional advancement professional becomes one:

first, by self-evaluation of personal traits, talents and skills required;

second, by step-by-step growth in the process of applied experience;

third, by careful observation and listening to policies, procedures, practice and results;

fourth, by personal interpretation of those observations;

fifth, by observing others in their implementation of related functions at peer and competing institutions;

sixth, by becoming students dedicated to developing the art of the advancement process; and

seventh, by becoming students of the philosophy, psychology, and spiritual essence of philanthropy, including the motivations of people who share their time, talents, and treasure.

This is quite an order. It is an order which mandates self-education. And self-education must take place even after attending all sorts of conferences, meetings, and courses.

Underlying all programs in the development or institution advancement function is the desire to get people to do something at or for the institution. To enroll in classes. To consider employment. To accept the responsibility of trusteeship. To give time as volunteers. To award grants. To attend special events. To become better advocates for the institution. To share a portion of annual income for annual support. To share some portion of current assets for special programs or projects. To include the institution in estate plan provisions beginning now with a planned gift. There is nothing in this tabulation which offers people anything tangible. People must come to or give to the institution for an intangible or personally perceived benefit. There is no product to hold in a person's hand as a symbol of a purchase, a policy or any benefit. Yes, under certain conditions, a person may receive a computer enrollment card, a certificate, a ticket stub, and sometimes even a thank you letter.

The point is that getting people to do something at or for the institution is a sales function with an intangible benefit to the doer or the donor. Newcomers to the development field must examine themselves in terms of their capability and tolerance in being part of a sales organization which has no tangible product. What traits or motivations does each newcomer possess which assure comfiture, confidence, and zeal to perfect those traits and motivations to the highest order for consummate personal satisfaction? Only you can answer that.

In terms of financial support, we deal in the utmost intangible personal motivation. One has to experience the quiet, contemplative satisfactions evident in a donor's countenance to know why he or she has made a significant gift. There is a dignified, spiritual satisfaction expressed without words. It is these analyses and satisfactions that aspiring professionals experience as they go on in their work, higher in responsibility, broader in perspective, and greater in philanthropic accomplishment.

First, evaluate yourself. Given these analyses of sales, philanthropic perspective, and time for experience, are you willing to apply, bend, stretch your talents and skills for these purposes for your institution, for its constituents, for your own pleasure and growth?

Second, train yourself. Do your assigned job better because you want to, not just because a manager says that you must. Proving that you can is personal growth. Beat the time schedule, be ahead of time for appointments, produce better thought-out work in getting ready for the next step up.

Third, listen and hear. Listening without hearing is an unsung national disease. Analyze who did what, why, and how. Study the process, the receiver, and the results to your own understanding of the why of what happened. Then think what could have been done better for greater and faster results.

Fourth, given what you have learned and observed, studied and analyzed, interpret those findings to your own experience. What will you do in the same situation given the opportunity? Witnessing life without partaking in it and improving it is personal waste.

Fifth, look around you and see what others are doing in similar situations. Yes, observe the competition. They're observing you. You both can learn and build and create and grow.

Sixth, study and read whatever you can wherever you can about the development process. Much has been written. Much has been said. But not so much as in other service fields that you cannot learn what was, learn what is, and then create what will be.

Seventh, no professional is merely an accomplished mechanic. True professionals are students of and practitioners of the philosophy, the psychology, the history, the traditions, and the motivations of their field. Mechanics provide the steak — the substance for action.

The development professional inspires others and leads the way in confidence that he/she knows what he/she knows because he/she has been there. The true professional will be respected for his/her sophisticated confidence; knowledge from study, observation, interpretation, experience; proofs of past results. And fellow officers, staff, faculty, students, friends, families, businesses, and foundation staff will listen and heed the professional as he/she points the way toward greater advancement.

There is no place for arrogance, human insensitivity, egoists, impatience, self-glory or martyrs in the philanthropic development field.

Let us all join with humility in the studied ministry of philanthropy, devoting our talents and skills that others may benefit from our quiet professionalism.

Evaluating an Institutional Advancement Program

There is no magical way to evaluate the success of an institutional advancement program. From the beginning, the advancement function is a sequence of events in the artful management of people and design of programs to motivate people — from the planning stage to obtaining a financial commitment in writing from people and organizations who want to share their assets for the benefit of others.

The first satisfactions and rewards of accomplishment are qualitative. A small gift from a difficult, even recalcitrant prospect, may provide greater reward and promise of greater potential than raising 15 percent more than last year's annual fund. The commitment of 10 planned gifts where there may have been none could provide the greatest hope for the future. Yet, trustees, treasurers, and staff erroneously belief that the development function can be measured only in terms of annual cash funds in hand. Such a belief is unreasonable unless preconditions are well planned and well implemented by all concerned.

Evaluation begins with expectancy. Miracles do not "just happen" in administration, in sales or in philanthropic giving; they must be engineered. Only to the extent to which they are engineered with reason, patience, thoroughness, commitment, understanding, and hard work can they be measured. Success doesn't just happen.

Productivity is an elusive criterion, whether applied to direct or indirect services, research, business operations or general administration. The organizational development officer, however, is in a particularly vulnerable position for testing by fact rather than by hope. It is mandatory, therefore, that the criteria for judgment be fair to all.

The development officer and the development program will not suffer low productivity rating if:

1. the organization is ready or intends to get ready for a progressively aggressive philanthropic sales program, sometimes requiring as many three years to mature;

2. the positions and functions are properly described to, planned for, and implemented under active trustee implementation;
3. the development personnel candidates are thoroughly researched before retention as to proven sensitivity, personality, and executive sales capacity not "just experience" in moving from one job to another;
4. the trustees, all administrators, all staff leaders understand the teamwork requirements for *total organizational success,* not just development office success;
5. the internal and support constituencies — public relations, news bureau, publications personnel — understand that their function is justified only in terms of payoff in the resource development program for both leadership and financial support as the payoff for greater understanding, awareness, interest, and concern.

The organization will have degrees of failure in its development program:

1. if 100 percent of the members of the governing board are not consistent, proportionate contributors to the annual fund program — a part of the required budget income which they approve in advance;
2. if 100 percent of the sponsoring groups, development councils or committees are not contributors to the annual fund;
3. if 100 percent of the senior administrators are not contributors to the annual fund;
4. if the annual fund is not an organization-wide record of annual support as a central gift receiving and accountability fund for annually recurring gifts;
5. if the top 100 prospects are not identified and researched and studied as to interests and potential;
6. if the most promising 10 percent are not carefully studied and scheduled for involvement and communication, and the top one percent are not identified and researched for very special handling;

7. if a planned giving (deferred gift) program is not established in the first year and sustained creatively in nearly all media;
8. if all publications and communications maintain a business-as-usual posture omitting promotional articles, statements, and reports on financial need requirements, gifts received, volunteer leadership, and the role of private sector support;
9. if development office personnel view their job as essentially internal rather than external;
10. if receipt, recording, and acknowledgment procedures for donations require more than 48 hours;
11. if the records and research office is not adequate to meet information retrieval requirements of volunteers and staff;
12. if too many people must "approve" the case statement and promotional materials;
13. if the case for support is not 100 percent supported by facts, financial integrity, constituency expectancy;
14. if public advocacy of the organization's importance and urgency for support is shunned by trustees, top volunteers, staff, and constituent leaders;
15. if volunteer leadership is enlisted for their names' sake rather than for action-oriented influence and affluence benefit as authenticators and advocates;
16. if volunteers defer and delay committed responsibilities;
17. if the chief executive shunts top prospect conditioning and solicitation responsibilities to lowest priority;
18. if business officers interfere in the administration and reporting responsibilities of the development officer;
19. if administrative planning for meetings, telephone follow-ups, minutes of meetings, and a myriad of details are sloppy and considered unimportant;
20. if meetings, office hours, and appointments are not kept and respected;
21. if other administrative responsibilities and/or off-site counsel jobs interfere with staff members' prime responsibility;
22. if time schedules and goals are not set and adhered to;

23. if staff, trustee or volunteer egos dominate both experience and judgment; that is, if "I, me, and my" get in the way of "we and us";
24. if professional or academic discipline training prevents expansive programs and opportunities; and
25. if telephone switchboard operators and secretaries are curt, impersonal, and insensitive to callers.

Only three or four of the above points refer to dollars directly, but each does indirectly. Confidence in the competence of management is one of the greatest motivators for staff associates, volunteers, and donors alike to work, work hard; give and give again.

The achievement of dollar goals is the product of the successful handling of countless details of administration in preparation, implementation, and follow-up. Evaluation of success by dollars alone without consideration of ground prepared for next year is both hollow and invalid. The billiard champion is not so much concerned with the ball at play as he is for setting up his next play.

In summary, the evaluation of a development program is the sum total of a great many details. Unappreciated opportunities to interest and impress people abound. These opportunities, consciously and conscientiously executed continuously, will make the dollar objectives for annual and capital funds and asset giving far easier to achieve and will make larger endowment possible sooner.

Man holds in his hands through life and hereafter only that which he has given away. Our test should be the tests of man's love expressed to his fellow man, which will provide many warm returns — even dollars.

Thoughtful Questions for a Philanthropic Prospect

In considering making a major gift, every prospective donor-investor must receive a "yes" to the following questions:

1. Does the cited need really exist and depend upon a financial resolution?
2. Is the organization experienced for the kind of resolution proposed by the financial request?
3. Does the organization have a clear vision of the results desired from fulfillment of the proposed request?
4. What is the expertise of the chief executive officer and related staff of the organization in philathropy and what have been their results?
5. How solid is the organization financially?
6. Does the organization have the facilities, personnel, and expertise to implement the plan and the philanthropic process?
7. Is the gift request comprehensible, with only a few technical, legal or gift process requirements?

Adapted from the joy and disappointments of George N. Boone and his wife Mary Lou in their new world — discovering the joy of giving. *Advancing Philanthropy,* Spring 1994, the National Society of Fund Raising Executives.

❧ 5 ☙
The Methods of
Accountability

The nonprofit board chair responsibility is a human condition, not created by divine authority.

Bylaws are the management guidelines for the administration of board governance policies.

Philanthropy is a business, and much more. It embraces hopes and dreams, it is a personal trust, it tests the integrity of the organization and the good will of everyone involved. Any act of philanthropy, any governance of a nonprofit organization must be way beyond reproach.

There should be no shortage of guidelines, checklists, policy statements, rules, and procedures. All must be considered and many ignored. Each organization and each leadership group has its own distinctive needs, problems, strengths, and weaknesses, and the tools of accountability should be designed accordingly.

Still, it is helpful to have some models from which to fashion whatever tools are needed, so here are a few.

The Structure of
Nonprofit Organization Bylaws

A Perspective

The preparation of bylaws or their reconstruction should be a major administrative project with the appointment of every new board chair and chief executive officer.

These management guidelines are important to every board member candidate, every inducted trustee, to guide personal service, and confidence-building as rules of operation.

Seldom have I seen copies of bylaws which show acceptance by the board. Seldom is acceptance dated. Seldom are officers shown as verifiers of board acceptance. Seldom are bylaws relevant to today's rapid economic and social changes. Seldom are bylaws constructed by experienced nonprofit management counsellors. Yet, the existence of authentic, comprehensive, relevant, official *management guidelines* as bylaws are as crucial as Robert's Rules of Order in parliamentary procedures.

Having been involved in almost countless nonprofit governance matters, membership reconstruction, and resultant bylaw reorganization, the following have been implemented by such clients who have lived happier ever after.

Sample Nonprofit Organization Bylaws: Management Guidelines for Governance

ARTICLE 1. AUTHORITY.

SECTION 1:1 FOUNDING. [Cite the occasion, purpose, and relationships for founding the organization without citing its entire history.]

SECTION 1:2 INCORPORATION. [Cite the reference to appropriate not-for-profit corporate statutes of the incorporating state, the date of the incorporation, and the date of the letter from the Internal Revenue Service citing the nature of the tax-exempt status.]

SECTION 1:3 NAME. The name of the corporation for all legal purposes is _____ .

SECTION 1:4 PRINCIPAL OFFICE. The office of the corporation at which the general business of the corporation will be transacted and the records of the corporation will be kept shall be at such place as may be determined by the Board of Trustees.

SECTION 1:5 TERM. The term of the existence for the organization is perpetual.

SECTION 1:6 FISCAL YEAR. The fiscal year of the organization shall be from _____ to _____ .

SECTION 1:7 REGISTERED AGENT. The organization shall have and continuously maintain at its principal office a registered agent to be designated by the Board of Trustees as the Chief Executive Officer of the corporation. The Secretary of the Board shall notify appropriate legal officers of the registered office and agent annually.

SECTION 1:8 RECORDS. The organization shall keep correct, complete, and up-to-date records of all management policies, personnel, services, programs, fiscal accounts, and inventories. The minutes and proceedings of the Governing Board, its committees and related units and departments shall be kept at its registered office. All records of the organization may be inspected by any member of the Governing Board or the member's agent or attorney for any proper purpose during business hours with appropriate advance approval.

SECTION 1:9 MEMBERS. Members of the corporation shall consist only of the members of the Board of Trustees.

SECTION 1:10 SEAL. The organization shall [shall not] have an official seal.

ARTICLE 2. THE BOARD OF TRUSTEES. The governance and the management of the organization shall be vested in a self-perpetuating Board of Trustees with responsibilities and obligations for policy management of a public trust under the auspices of state statutes, the articles of incorporation, and appropriate federal rules and regulations.

SECTION 2:1 MEMBERSHIP. The Board of Trustees shall be composed of no less than three (3) nor more than _____ . (_____) voting members shall be selected for their interest in, concern for, and personal commitment to participate effectively in fulfilling their responsibilities for managing a public trust.

SECTION 2:2 ELECTION. The committee on board management (formally called the nominating committee) shall be responsible for comprehensive and objective research for potential board members for all board functions, officers of the board, and for memberships in board-related categories. Such research shall be in accordance with studied and updated position descriptions for all functions. Such nominations shall be subject to approval of voting members of the Board of Trustees as appropriate, and, as provided for in these bylaws, at any regular meeting of the Governing Board.

SECTION 2:3 TERMS. Members of the Board of Trustees shall be elected for a term of four (4) years or to complete an unexpired term of a former member. No member shall be elected to more than two consecutive full terms. A member who completes an unexpired term by serving for less than two years may be elected to two full terms consecutive with the unexpired term. A member who completes an unexpired term by serving for two years or more may be elected to only one full term consecutive with the unexpired term. For the purposes of this section, terms are consecutive if they are less than one year apart.

SECTION 2:4 ROLE OF THE BOARD. The Board of Trustees shall:

a. fulfill the responsibilities contained in the state statutory requirements;

b. ensure that the purpose, mission, and goals cited in the articles of incorporation are accomplished;

c. study, establish, review, and evaluate periodically all policies set by the board;

d. elect members for limited terms as officers of the corporation;

e. select, appoint, evaluate, and support a Chief Executive Officer consistent with a realistic position description;

f. create a long-range plan for all services, programs, and fiscal stability and security of the organization; and

g. personally support and serve as a constant advocate of the mission and services of the organization.

SECTION 2:5 VACANCIES. The Board may fill any board member vacancy at any regular meeting upon recommendation of the standing committee on board management.

SECTION 2:6 EX OFFICIO STATUS. The Board and any of its committees may appoint individuals as ex officio members with Board approval and shall specify whether they are members with or without vote.

SECTION 2:7 HONORARY TRUSTEES. The Board may appoint honorary trustees who shall not have served as regular voting trustees but whose positions render authentication and validity of the mission of the organization. There shall be a position description, term of service, and attendance at Board and committee meetings citing their ex officio role as with or without vote.

SECTION 2:8 EMERITI TRUSTEES. Trustees who have served the organization with distinction may be appointed trustees emerti. The Board shall prepare a position description, including their ex officio role as with or without vote in attending Board and committee meetings.

SECTION 2:9 REPRESENTATION. No member of the Governing Board is authorized to represent any discussion or decision of the Governing Board nor act as a personal representative of the Board unless specifically authorized to do so.

SECTION 2:10 CHANNEL TO/FROM STAFF. All communications to and from any members of the Board of Trustees or to and from any members of the staff shall only be through the Chief Executive Officer.

SECTION 2:11 CONFLICT OF INTEREST. Any member of the Board of Trustees who has a direct or indirect financial or executive interest in any contract or transaction with the organization must disclose such interest to the Governing Board. The individual concerned may not participate in discussions or votes relating to the subject of their interest.

SECTION 2:12 INDEMNIFICATION. The organization may indemnify Governing Board members or staff officers for expenses and costs (including attorney's fees) actually and necessarily incurred by them in connection with any claim asserted against them, by action in court or otherwise, by reason of their being or having been such Governing Board members or officer, except in relation to matters as to which they shall have been guilty of negligence or misconduct in respect to the matter in which indemnity is sought.

ARTICLE 3. MEETINGS.

SECTION 3:1 REGULAR MEETINGS. The Board of Trustees shall meet regularly at least three (3) times each fiscal year at a time and place determined by the Board Chair and Chief Executive Officer with schedules arranged one (1) year in advance.

SECTION 3:2 ANNUAL MEETING. The annual meeting of the Board of Trustees shall be the last regular meeting held before the new fiscal year.

SECTION 3:3 SPECIAL MEETINGS. Special meetings may be called by the Board Chair, the Chief Executive Officer, or at the request of any five (5) voting members of the Board. The notice of such special meeting shall contain a statement of the purpose of such meeting. No other business shall be transacted at such meeting.

SECTION 3:4 NOTICE. A written notice stating the date, place, and time of Board meetings shall be sent by the Secretary at least ten (10) days before each meeting together with the proposed agenda and appropriate support materials of agenda items to be studied before the stated meeting.

SECTION 3:5 QUORUM. A quorum for the conduct of business shall consist of a majority of the voting members of the Board in office.

SECTION 3:6 PROXY. No attendance or voting by proxy is permitted.

SECTION 3:7 ACTION BY TELEPHONE CONFERENCE. Members of the Governing Board or any committee may participate in any meeting by means of telephone conference or similar communication equipment in which all persons participating can communicate with each other. Participation in a meeting pursuant to this section shall constitute presence in person at such meetings.

SECTION 3:9 EXECUTIVE SESSION. Any voting member of the Board of Trustees or its committees may call for a vote for an executive session and the Chair must then order.

SECTION 3:10 ORDER OF BUSINESS. The Board Chair, the Chief Executive Officer, and the Chair of the committee on board management shall consult each other on the preparation of relevant agenda items for Board meetings. Robert's Rules of Order, Revised, is adopted to govern procedures of the Board and its committees.

SECTION 3:11 ATTENDANCE. Any Board member who fails to attend two (2) consecutive regular meetings without explanation satisfactory to the committee on board management shall be considered to have resigned as member of the Board.

SECTION 3:12 TERMINATION. Any Board member may be terminated for cause by a vote of three-fourths (3/4) of the voting members of the Board.

SECTION 3:13 ORIENTATION. Every new member of the Governing Board must participate in a comprehensive, on-site, department-by-department, program-by-program orientation by appropriate personnel in order to ethically serve as a knowledgeable trustee in the formulation and evaluation of all policies.

SECTION 3:14 EXPENSES. All expenses incurred on behalf of attendance and participation in Board and committee meetings and events are tax deductible to members. Reimbursement for such expenses are not tax deductible.

ARTICLE 4. OFFICERS OF THE BOARD.

SECTION 4:1 OFFICERS. The Officers of the Corporation shall be Officers of the Governing Board. The Officers shall be a Chair, one Vice Chair, Secretary, and Treasurer each of whom shall be regular, voting members of the Board. Except for the Chair, all officers may serve also as Chairs of Standing committees. Officers shall be elected each year by a majority vote of the

Board, but shall serve for no more than three (3) years. Officer vacancies shall be filled by the Board at the first regular meeting held after the vacancy occurs.

SECTION 4:2 CHAIR. The Board Chair shall preside at all meeings of the Board of Trustees and of the Executive Committee, when possible, and shall be ex officio member without vote of all committees except the Committee on Board Management. The Chair shall be responsible for active leadership of and among Board members in discharging its powers, responsibilities, and obligations as a public trust.

SECTION 4:3 VICE CHAIR. The Vice Chair shall have all powers and duties of the Chair during the absence, disability or disqualification of the Chair.

SECTION 4:4 THE SECRETARY. The Board Secretary shall execute all legal matters of the organization, cause the notices and minutes of all Governing Board and Executive Committee meetings to be prepared, recorded and distributed, and shall certify the accuracy of such documents and records; shall attest to the signatures of Officers of the Corporation and Governing Board; and shall cause the policies adopted by the Governing Board to be maintained in a Board of Trustees Policy Manual available at all meetings.

SECTION 4:5 THE TREASURER. The Treasurer, who may also serve as Chair of the Committee on Financial Affairs, shall have custody of all funds, securities, and other fiduciary resources belonging to the organization, except those committed to the custody of others by action of the Governing Board. The Treasurer shall have access to records of all receipts, disbursements, assets, and liabilities of the organization and shall report to the Governing Board on the condition of such records and financial condition of the organization at the regular Board meetings. For the annual meeting of the Board, the Treasurer shall insure that an annual operating budget and report on the financial condition be presented to the Board of Trustees for their approval and personal support. At the close of the fiscal year, the Treasurer shall cause to be prepared an outside audit report on the financial status of the organization and a report on the adequacy of internal controls. The treasurer shall cause all appropriate employees of the organization to be adequately bonded.

SECTION 4:6 ASSISTANT SECRETARY and ASSISTANT TREASURER. The Board of Trustees shall appoint, upon recommendation of the Chief Executive Officer, staff persons to assist the Board Secretary and Board Treasurer in the fulfillment of their duties but who shall not be members of the Board.

SECTION 4:7 COMPENSATION. No Officer or member of the Governing Board shall receive compensation for services as Officer or member of the Corporation or Board of Trustees.

ARTICLE 5. COMMITTEES OF THE BOARD. The Board of Trustees shall function through standing and/or special or ad hoc committees in the conduct of the purposes and business of the organization. Neither the Governing Board nor the Executive Committee shall act first on matters properly within the responsibilities of standing, special or ad hoc committees for their recommendations, except in emergencies.

SECTION 5:1 THE EXECUTIVE COMMITTEE. This committee shall consist of all Officers of the Board of Trustees and Chairs of all standing committees. The Executive Committee shall have all powers of the Governing Board between meetings of that Board except the encumbrance of property, reversal of previous Board actions, to fiscally obligate the organization in any way, or employ or remove, the Chief Executive Officer. The Chief Executive Officer shall serve as staff to this committee.

SECTION 5:2 STANDING COMMITTEES. The membership of standing committees shall be named at the annual meeting of the Board of Trustees. Appointment shall be made annually by the Chair of the Board upon recommendation of the committee on board management. Members shall serve until their successors are appointed. Committee chairs may appoint subcommittees of voting members, usually three (3), and which may include persons not members of the Board as ex officio members without vote.

The responsibility of each standing committee shall be to develop and recommend specific courses of action and to propose policies to assure that the public trust responsibilities and mission fulfillment objectives of the organization are implemented. This will be done through:

a. familiarizing itself with goals and objectives, procedures and programs, staff and facilities;

b. monitoring progress toward short- and long-term objectives;

c. identify issues, trends, and forces which should be brought to the attention of the Governing Board; and

d. analyzing issues which require Board action.

The standing committees shall include the committees on board management, financial affairs, resource development, and programs and services.

SECTION 5:3 MEETINGS. Standing, special, and/or ad hoc committee meetings shall be held at the call of the committee Chair or by the Chief Executive Officer but shall meet at least three (3) times each fiscal year.

SECTION 5:4 THE COMMITTEE ON BOARD MANAGEMENT. This committee has the responsibility to assist the Board of Trustees in ensuring that individual and joint responsibilities for managing a public trust are accomplished fully. The committee prepares statements on the role of the Governing Board, board position descriptions, criteria of membership, evaluation of personal commitments of members, research on nominees and candidates, and recommendations for functional appointments.

The functions of this committee shall include but not be limited to: maintaining a list of potential trustees, nominating trustees for election, studying the changing needs of the organization assessing Board operation, structure, and attendance to assure maximum effectiveness and efficiency; assisting in designing special Board events and retreats; providing for the comprehensive orientation of new members, and recommendation for the disinvitation of present Board members. The Chief Executive Officer or staff nominee shall staff this committee.

SECTION 5:5 THE FINANCIAL AFFAIRS COMMITTEE. Under the authority of the policies and procedures established by the Governing Board, this committee shall have responsibilities to plan, implement, report, and evaluate all policies, procedures, and programs relating to personnel positions, salaries, and benefits, and to retain counsellors for investments, insurance, physical plant, and audits. The Chair may appoint investment, audit, physical plant, and other subcommittees as appropriate. The Treasurer of the Board shall be Chair of this committee. The Chief Executive Officer shall designate a staff person to serve as staff to this committee.

SECTION 5:6 THE RESOURCE DEVELOPMENT COMMITTEE. This committee shall be responsible for the following administrative operations: public relations, publicity, marketing, membership, and philanthropic gift and grant programs for current budget support, special programs, and endowment. The Chief Executive Officer shall appoint a staff person to serve as staff for this committee.

SECTION 5:7 THE COMMITTEE ON PROGRAMS AND SERVICES. This committee shall be responsible for assisting in the planning, implementation, and evaluation of all programs, projects, and services of the organization. The Chief Executive Officer shall appoint a staff person to serve as staff for this committee.

SECTION 5:8 SPECIAL COMMITTEES. From time to time, the Board Chair may appoint special or ad hoc committees to study and make recommendations to the Board for special problems, projects or services. The term of such committees shall not exceed one year. The Chair of such committees shall always be a voting member of the Board of Trustees. The Chief Executive Officer shall appoint a person to serve as staff for these committees.

ARTICLE 6. THE ADMINISTRATION.

SECTION 6:1 AUTHORITY AND RESPONSIBILITY. The Governing Board Chair together with the Chief Executive Officer form a management partnership in fulfilling the mission of the organization.

SECTION 6:2 THE CHIEF EXECUTIVE OFFICER. The Chief Executive Officer shall be the Chief Administrator of the organization, who shall be:

a. primary spokesperson for the organization;
b. accountable for implementing and monitoring board policies and recommending future policies;
c. responsible for continual long-range planning;
d. primary liaison with the Board of Trustees, its committees, volunteers, and channel to and from the Board and staff;
e. responsible for enlisting and maintaining executive staff, fair personnel policies, and a plan of organization;
f. a member of the Governing Board without vote; and
g. responsible for preparation of operating budgets, special programs, grant requests, endowment for fiscal stability and security, personnel

policies, and all relations, marketing, and re-source development operations.

SECTION 6:3 DISTRIBUTION. Copies of these Bylaws shall be made available immediately to all members of the Governing Board, Executive Officers, appropriate staff, and legal entities as appropriate. The Articles of Incorporation shall be distributed and included with these bylaws.

ARTICLE 7. AMENDMENT OF BYLAWS. These Bylaws may be amended from time to time by the Board of Trustees at any regular meeting of the Board provided that such proposed changes be sent to voting members of the Board at least 30 days prior thereto. A majority of the voting members present shall be required for adoption of changes.

CERTIFICATE

We certify that the foregoing is a true copy of the Bylaws of this organization approved at a regular meeting of the Board of Trustees on _____ 19 ____ and in effect as of this date.

Date: _____ 19 ____ .

Chair   Secretary
The Organization   The Organization
Board of Trustees   Board of Trustees

The Committee on Board Management — The Managing Group for Managers

Trustees are a disadvantaged segment of our society. Governing boards are substantially unmanaged to perform responsibilities their statutory legal obligations require. Most state statutes indicate that governing board members are responsible for managing (not administering) a public trust on behalf of the people of the incorporating state for the public good as not-for-profit corporations. Immediately the question arises as to whom the responsibility falls for the administration of the management group of individuals who constitute the governing board. Normally this responsibility falls to the organization's chief executive officer (CEO) who becomes simultaneously the administrative officer of the governing board. Seldom are the functions of the administrative officer of the board defined anywhere. Before recommending a solution to the governing board management vacuum, let's examine current options prevalent among our nation's not-for-profit organizations.

CEO Perceptions

The administrative style of chief executive officers as they view their relationship to governing boards falls into four categories:

Category One. Keep your distance. This style of administration resents the presence of the governing board as likely to interfere with the chief executive's administration of the board's management policies. This happens even in view of the fact that that very governing board has retained, should evaluate periodically, and can discharge the chief executive officer. Here, ego dominates both confidence and reason. Such chief executive officers tread upon dangerous ground were it not for the collateral fact that governing boards who retain such staff executives are also willing to abdicate continuous management responsibilities until a crisis arises.

That "distance" from intimate involvement is characterized by having only one or two board meetings each fiscal year, no committee meetings (or few), absence of substance in meeting agenda, sporadic communications or "tons" of irrelevant paper, little or no personal attention to board members of influence and/or affluence, and refusal to permit staff officers to communicate with board members or to staff properly committees related to the staff function.

Occasionally, a chief executive officer is such an outstanding administrator that the organization does function spectacularly without intimate board involvement. In nearly 50 years of dealing with the not-for-profit sector, only one such chief executive can be cited. Usually under this style of board administration, board members become apathetic about the organization or drop off to look for stimulating experiences elsewhere — and they should.

Category Two. Let's build together. Administrators who are talented in human relations, administration, and are committed to the long-term growth and development of the organization, view governing board members as partners in policy design, policy management, and policy implementation. This partnership begins with creating sensitive relationships (and training if necessary) between staff officers and related board committees. The partnership is extended by bringing board members "into" the organization (not merely above it) for long-range planning, budget building, and other participatory functions. Therefore, board members get to know the people, programs, facilities, problems, potential, and policies necessary for quality performance as well as for future stability and security.

While governing boards are admonished never to cross the line between policy setting and policy implementation, strong boards are developed by clear delineations of role and function and by involvement before policies are recommended for eventual adoption and implementation. Thus grounded in mutual respect for differing roles, the partnership can mature for the full satisfaction of all concerned. Here, even those governing board members who have limited time for such involvement will make time for the personal fulfillment achieved. Committee meetings and board meetings will become more interesting because members know the organization, understand its people, appreciate its services, become strong advocates, ask constructive questions, and provide and seek substantial financial support.

Category Three. Count me in. Chief executive officers who demand full governing board membership even though they are employees of that board advertise their presumptive ego as well as their distrust of board functions without their own vote being counted. In these situations, the function of the board agenda and action becomes awkward to design and implement objectively. Proposed policy recommendations of the chief executive are voted on by that chief executive thereby placing the individual in the position of being prosecuting attorney and jury. With this kind of arrangement, it is impossible for governing boards to have executive sessions for assessing the chief executive performance or other policy action or review matters. Where CEOs are voting board members, governing board members tend to defer to their own member (the CEO) in all matters because of the position, role, and function of chief executive officer. Individual initiative, concern, and full commitment becomes thwarted by the voting presence of the CEO and the governing board begins to float into apathy.

Category Four. It's already decided. Too many governing board meetings are rubber stamp sessions. Chief executives, staff officers, and/or board committee chairpersons merely report on what happened since the last meeting. No greater insult to personal integrity, interest, concern, and capacity for executive, entrepreneurial, volunteer leadership exists when board members are relegated to positions of puppets motioning and seconding actions of which they have precious little knowledge of importance, impact or implications.

Thus it is that governing boards are more to be pitied than censured for increasing apathy, reluctant advocacy, and invisible financial support.

Board Management Constraints. How many organizations have governing boards which have studied their reason for being, from examining the state, federal, and Internal Revenue Service incorporation documents to organizational long-range planning operations? Few, very few. The question, "Is this board really necessary?" — is it a relevant and legitmate one? Are more than the statutory required number of members really necessary? Why? To what purpose? Even the answers to these and numerous other questions are illegitimate if only revalidation of the status quo results. Governing boards should be subjected to rigorous, objective, experienced self-study periodically. Such self-studies should be directed, even staffed, by thoroughly experienced counsellors. And such counsellors most probably should not be former chief executives unless careful examination reveals that their own board management and administrative practices have objectively proven to be exemplary.

Position Description. Seldom can there be found organizations which have related the functions and purposes of the organization to the requirements for identifying and enlisting new board members. Governing board position descriptions are virtually nonexistent. Descriptions of desired personal characteristics and personal qualities are mandatory. Unless an organization knows why it wants board members, what it wants them to be, what it wants them to do, it is flying blind. A thorough self-study could provide the basis for greatly enhancing the quality of board members.

Nominating Committee. Perhaps there is no greater farce in the management of not-for-profit organizations than the presumed function of the average nominating committee. Usually its membership consists of those individuals who were dysfunctional elsewhere on the board and/or those who have been on the board too long. Further, its only function usually is performed two or three weeks before an annual meeting: The nominating committee chair calls the chief executive officer to ask who to put on the board, who to renominate, and who to graduate off the board. This crucial process usually results in friends of present board members being enthusiastically nominated because "they are such nice people." And so, those nice people get asked, are elected, "serve" or are served, and press on in meaningless roles.

Enlistment Process. The governing board enlistment process is usually casual, complimentary, indefinite, and without real substance. Friends approaching friends for board membership is a relatively easy task where availability is the only matter of concern. Seldom are candidates tested as to their interests in the organization's mission; seldom are they given copies of the incorporating state statutes or articles of incorporation or bylaws; seldom are the full, expected responsibilities explained in detail before enlistment, and seldom are candidates with their spouses asked or required to personally visit every office, facility or function to be able to act knowledgeably on board matters. Nice people just gather to ask nice people to do nice things.

Cloistered Meetings. Board and committee meetings are usually held in special rooms reserved for board functions. Why not have such meetings in the action-oriented places within the organization to see and to be seen? Most trustees need labels on their clothing to be identified as such. Seldom do trustees get to see the "inside" of the organization. A trustee-in-residence program should require new trustees to visit each office, each service area, each major program within 90 days of becoming a trustee, or withdraw the appointment. Meetings of individual trustees should be one-on-one, not group sessions. General board meetings should be staged and constructed in different environments, with different types of agenda, with different features relevant to the organization's function, including guest speakers as appropriate. Each such meeting should be a learning experience, not just a dull reporting session.

And there are more constraints that seriously affect trustee performance negatively. But the question comes down to what to do about all the above management deficiences.

Create a Committee on Board Management

Eliminate the nominating committee! Create a committee on board management with this bylaw statement as the first cited standing committee:

The functions of this committee shall include but not be limited to:

1. designing a position description of basic, necessary personal and social characteristics required to meet the need, role, function, criteria, membership, expectations, obligations, and responsibilities; comprehensive bylaw management guidelines and evaluation criteria of the board and its members;

2. maintain a substantial, studied trustee candidate list — through a constant search to identify and to research those individuals best able to serve the nonprofit's mission, goals, and objectives and the organization at the governance level;

3. evaluate continually and appraise board organization, operation, membership participation level, personal gift support, and attendance to assure maximum

effectiveness and to make recommendations that, in its judgment, will accomplish the objectives of the governing board and the responsibilities of statutory laws; study continually the changing needs of the organization to assure that membership of the governing board reflects new talent, skills, experience, interests, leverage, affluence, influence, and other characteristics required for policy considerations, adoption and maintenance; responsibility for disinvitation of members who are not or who cannot fulfill minimum membership requirements; assistance in designing agenda, special events, presentations, and retreats to assess all forces, issues, and trends affecting or likely to affect the organization; and prepare and initiate a comprehensive plan for the orientation of new members of the governing board on site, and other bodies of the organization.

The chief executive officer shall be the staff resource person for this committee (along with the staff secretary and/or resource development officer as appropriate). The board chairperson must not be a member of this committee even ex officio!

With this outline of functions, the most crucial next steps include:

1. placing on this committee the most important, active, vital, concerned members of the governing board;
2. placing the importance of this committee second only to the executive committee;
3. staffing this committee as if the entire future of the organization depended upon the function of this committee with nominations of individuals as candidates, planning careful, sensitive, and thorough research on the candidates, and planning a strategy for each to "test" potential productivity.
4. planning careful, sensitive, and thorough research on the candidates; and
5. planning a strategy for each to test potential productivity.

Thus described and functioning, this committee becomes by far the most important committee of the governing board. They hold in their hands the power to affect the destiny of the organization forever in terms of their management of the board. And that management requires wisdom, commitment, judgment, ethics, morals, and just plain guts. The guts factor must be exercised by inviting members to vacate their position. This is not the responsibility of the chairperson of the board nor of the chief executive officer. It is the problem of the entire board. It is safe to estimate that 20 to 30 percent of each board is ineffective for whatever reason.

Governing board positions must be weighed as carefully as if each represented a one-million-dollar gift to the organization each year. When the value of the individual trustee measures up to expectations of interest, concern, and participation, fine. When that value must be excused, rationalized or otherwise equivocated, the organization proceeds into a question of its integrity or moral commitment to a dynamic future. This responsibility for effective trusteemanship is the task for the governing board itself — the committee on board management, the board's own management vehicle.

In planning its work, this committee should:

1. prepare and update regularly a statement on general and personal responsibilities and characteristics as an expression of policy and aspiration for board membership;
2. prepare a checklist for governing board member evaluation;
3. prepare a trustee position description.

The effective operation of such a management committee can make a board chair as well as the chief executive officer look very good. The committee exists to serve each as well as the board as a whole and the organization as it purports to serve society.

Trustees individually and as a whole body are in desperate need of help — management help, tender loving care of, by, and for its own membership from its own membership.

This committee is the answer properly mandated in bylaws, properly constituted with proven leadership individuals, properly staffed, and fully functional.

In the beginning and ultimately the future viability of each nonprofit organization rests in the hands and hearts of governing board — at law and in the focus of serving as a public trust.

> *The only way to predict*
> *the future is to have*
> *power to shape the future.*
> *— Eric Hoffer*

Every nonprofit organization knows that one-third of its governing board membership will be non-functional. In spite of careful plans for creating dedicated board members; in spite of studied position descriptions for board members; and in spite of strategic personal contacts for nuturing interest, orientation, and commitment, the "Rule of Thirds" will take effect.

That rule says that "among any group of people, one-third will perform as requested far beyond expectations, one-third will respond only to a liberal application of a rusty needle; and, one-third will not respond as requested or committed." Upon enlistment, no one knows who will fall into which third. Adding numbers of board members will only create more problems of both managers and administrators. That one-third rule is immortal.

The organization, the board itself, should require a written commitment from every new board member that he or she understands the role, function, purpose, obligation, responsibility, and accountability of each member. There must be a pledge, a statement of commitment, a letter of understanding from the members certifying in writing that they are aware of the public trust role and will honor that role and their personal relationship.

To these ends the following Statement of Understanding is offered as a guide for a complete mutual respect of personal expectations of the board as a whole and the individual new members.

Governing Board Member Statement of Understanding

Having considered the invitation to become a member of the board of trustees, having accepted the invitation, and having been inducted officially as a term member of the board of this organization, I am hereby fully committed and dedicated to the vision and mission of the organization. I hereby pledge to do my full part to ensure, even to insure, fulfillment of the mission. From the board and board member position descriptions, I understand that my duties, responsibilities, and obligations include the following:

1. The founding of the organization as a public trust is rooted in the not-for-profit corporate statutes of the incorporating state.
2. I am hereby personally and jointly responsible, with other board members, for the operation of this organization in fulfillment of its mission for humanitarian purposes.
3. I will be aware of the proposed and approved operating budget and also what the budget ought to be to ensure the highest quality in all programs, services, facilities, equipment, and staff requirements.
4. I pledge to do my part in actively reviewing and monitoring the budget through periodic reports and seeking necessary financial support to insure a balanced annual budget at least.
5. I am responsible to see, know, and oversee the implementation and implications of past and present board policies and programs.
6. I understand and will follow the governing board bylaws as management guidelines in fulfillment of the reputation of the organization.

7. I want to visit each principal officer, office, program, function, and staff member to see how and who is responsible for the functioning of the organization.
8. I will provide what is for me a substantial annual gift for budget operations. I will participate in special events. I will consider capital fund and estate gifts as appropriate for me.
9. I will actively promote this organization among all business friends, neighbors and family to encourage their support.
10. I will engage actively in cultivaton of friends for their generous support of our diverse activities, programs, and opportunities in the name of philanthropy.
11. I will attend board meetings, serve on committees as appropriate, and be available in person and by phone.
12. In signing this document I understand that there are no rigid standards of measurement or achievement for board members. This pledge is a statement of faith and trust among one another to perform to the best of our abilities.

The Certificate of Appointment will be a treasured honor.

Date   Name
                         Address
                         Phone

In its turn, this organization is responsible to me as follows:

1. I will receive financial and appropriate dated reports regularly which I will read before meetings.
2. I will be able to discuss policies, programs, goals, objectives, and perceptions with staff members through the chief executive officer.

3. Board members and staff will respond to the best of their ability in straightforward, honest, moral, ethical, legal, and fiscal responsibilities as members of a public trust.

Board Chair   Chief Executive Officer
Date   Date

Guidelines for Establishing Gift and Grant Policies

Every nonprofit organization must have basic governing board philanthropic gift and grant policies. These policies must concern the planning, promotion, solicitation, receipt, acceptance, management, reporting, use, and disposition of private sector resources in which no goods, services or direct benefits are expected, implied or forthcoming for the donor. The donors are expected to be individuals, couples, families, business firms, foundations or other organizations. This statement suggests basic guidelines for the creation of specific board policies but is not all-inclusive.

I. **General Concerns.** The objective consideration, adoption, implementation, and periodic evaluation of approved policies must be designed to:

A. protect the organization's tax-exempt status from possible abuse by donors and from retribution by state authorities or the U.S. Internal Revenue Service;
B. ensure that all donors are treated fairly and equally with personal credit only for personal gifts provided; business firms, foundations, and organizations must be credited specifically and separately for their gifts;

C. ensure that the governing board exercises its state statutory public trust responsibility in making final decisions for the acceptance of all gifts and for any exception to its policies and guidelines; administrators only receive gifts;

D. prevent the organization from being "used" as an object of philanthropic intent for either designed or innocent avoidance of taxes, prejudiced purposes, or evaluation of gifts without generous, advanced, objective, experienced evaluation;

E. provide authority for administrators to decline unacceptable gift offers by setting an example of doing so;

F. maximize, not substitute or diminish, its philanthropic potential from each separate constituency — each taxable entity, thereby

> 1.) eliminating duplicate credit; e.g., giving chief executive officers personal credit and personal recognition for business firm "cost of business" (100% tax deductible) grants or gift committee/business foundation commitments;
>
> 2.) eliminating substitute credit for a single gift or grant; e.g., giving a business firm chief executive personal credit for his/her firm's gift or grant but not recognizing the firm; or giving a volunteer cash gift credit for volunteer time provided, etc.;
>
> 3.) eliminating discount philanthropy; e.g., giving gift club credit for amounts less than the actual amount of the gift club minimum; and
>
> 4.) eliminating cash gift credit for gifts-in-kind whether or not relevant to the programs and services of the organization.

G. ensure that no board, volunteer or staff member is authorized to solicit philanthropic commitments without *a priori* knowledge of it by the chief executive officer and/or clearance with the resource development officer to prevent duplicate, uncoordinated presentations and organizational embarrassment;

H. ensure that all requests for gifts or grants are made within ethical business, professional, and philanthropic promotional practices avoiding even apparent conflicts of interest in present or future relationships;

I. ensure that organizational personnel shall not benefit personally by way of commission or other device related to gifts or grants received;

J. ensure that agreements, contracts, trusts, planned gift devices or other legal documents with any donor or sponsor are first approved by retained non-board member legal counsel; and

K. ensure that, where tax liability and/or estate consequences are a factor, such potential donors contact their own legal and/or tax counsellors.

II. **Definitions. Types of Gifts.** The governing board should recognize these forms of gift commitments:

A. **Unrestricted/Undesignated.** These gifts are urgent, necessary, and recurrent, to be used where the governing board deems best for the organization.

B. **Preferred Use (Designated).** Donors may indicate a preferred use of gifts but do not and will not hold the organization responsible for absolute, legal, restricted use which is cited only as a preference. When designated gifts are for budgeted items, they have the effect of being a "budget-relief" amount, substituting but not supplementing budget allocations. Therefore, they should be counted as current income — unrestricted gifts relieving budget allocations.

C. **Restricted/Legally Binding.** Such gifts should be few and far between inasmuch as they tie the hands of future governing boards should the purpose of the restriction no longer apply. No restricted gift should be accepted by the governing board without a "relief" statement such as the one which follows. This provision permits future governing boards to use such gifts nearest to the intent of the donor.

Relief Statement:
Should the purpose(s) for which this gift is provided no longer exist, the then existing governing board is authorized to apply the gift and/or its income nearest to the intended purpose.

D. **Gifts-in-Kind.** Gifts of equipment, supplies, professional services, contract services, art, furnishings, books, etc., should be accepted only if such gifts add materially to accomplishing the purposes of the organization. The IRS holds the donor responsible for evaluating the gift. The organization cannot be party to the evaluation. Such gifts, when requested from potential suppliers can save budget costs materially as well as provide urgently needed items not budgeted.

E. **Expectancies.** Commitments provided by bequest, estate plan or other deferred gift vehicles should be counted as expectancies when they are to "mature" at some future time. In many cases, donors and potential donors may change, increase or decrease their commitment depending upon how they are treated by the leadership of the organization as "future interest" donors. Eventual income from such commitments must never be counted in current/annual fund income amounts but, rather, counted "below the line" as with gifts-in-kind, investment income, property sale, and other income reports at their maturity value. Many organizations apply such income directly to endowment or use the income for urgent, non-budgeted but vital purposes. Evaluate the expected "donations" annually to accurately assess their impact on the organization and to give the donor credit for the gift.

F. **Capital Funds.** This popular term for resource development programs refers primarily to features and functions for organizational asset-building: endowed personnel positions, offices, programs, services, departments, units, and functions; equipment, library resources, furnishings, vehicles, tools, etc.;

human service features such as scholarships, patient health care; cultural functions; and physical plant requirements.

G. **Planned Gifts.** Personal and family commitments for current use and/or short-term or long-term endowment purposes may take many forms of deferred gift instruments. Planned giving means planning now for ultimate benefit to the organization. Therefore, a broad spectrum of donor investment gift opportunities (never totalled) must exist, to be scheduled at endowment amounts for income use at levels 10 years hence. The planned gift commitment assures that the given purpose will be "insured" by cash sometime later. Minimum endowment values, taking into account increasing administrative costs, must be reviewed annually. Deferred gift instrument minimums must also be reviewed annually because of dramatic changes in our national economy, rules, and regulations.

Firm future endowment commitments provide the opportunity for the donor to provide annually the interest on that endowment to serve its purpose now for the donor to see that it is working. This is a **functional endowment.**

H. **Gift Standards.** The following minimum standards should apply to naming physical facilities, programs, services, departments, and endowment objectives:

1.) physical facilities may be named for donors or as tributes or memorials only upon the assurance of receiving not less than 50 percent of total costs of that facility. Total costs include: architectural, planning, and construction costs; fees; site clearance and landscaping; furnishings; equipment; and endowment for future maintenance figured at 50 percent of total costs for general facilities and 100 percent for scientific facilities;

2.) named objectives for existing physical facilities should be figured at amounts of the value of the desired unit as a significant functional part of the physical plant;

3.) for executive positions, staff, programs, and functions, endowments must be cited at figures producing income for estimated total budgeted costs 10 years from now;

4.) donors of planned gifts should be recognized now and periodically in gift reports and newsletters by name or by the word "anonymous" where their name would appear alphabetically in a category called The Heritage Club or Legacy Associates or an honored name society, and the fees or costs for an annual event should be waived, to indicate that they are providing a future interest;

5.) an estimate of administrative costs for handling deferred gift instruments, property sales, research, etc., must be provided for as appropriate cost of handling the process (e.g., some organizations assess a general 15 percent; some universities assess a cost from 45 to 100 percent.)

III. **Suggested Policies.** The following features and factors should be considered as basic but must be reviewed every five years at least.

Policy #1. Legal. The organization shall accept only those gifts the transference and implementation of which shall be deemed consistent with public laws and/or regulations and/or public policy of the respective incorporating state and the federal government.

Policy #2. Purpose. The organization shall accept only those gifts which are consistent with the mission, goals, purposes, and services of the organization for the implementation and support of its accepted administrative practices and the pursuit of its programs of public service.

Policy #3. Authority. No individuals or unit of the organization shall solicit funds in the name of or on behalf of the organization until and unless authorized to do so by the governing board, the chief executive officer or their officially approved representative.

Policy #4. Clearance. Purposes for which funds shall be sought shall be cleared in advance of any solicitation of any potential donor by the chief executive officer of the organization.

Policy #5. Acceptance. Gifts, grants, and gift instruments may be received by the chief executive officer or his/her designee but can be accepted officially only by the governing board as managers of the public trust.

Policy #6. Gift Value. No individual in the employ of the organization shall verify the value of a gift in written form other than cash, checks or gifts-in-kind for tax deduction purposes. (See Policy #14 with reference to planned gift devices.)

Policy #7. Physical Plant Endowment. Physical plant facility costs — new, additions or modernized — shall include a cost for endowment of maintenance in perpetuity as an up-front cost, which is usually 50 percent of total basic turn-key costs.

Policy #8. Administrative Costs. All program and special service proposals shall include a percentage cost of administration and other overhead features as costs of implementation.

Policy #9. Named Endowments. To name a permanent endowment fund shall require a minimum gift of, say, $5,000. Such endowments may be carried as open-end funds for the later addition of resources. Donors should be requested to provide annual income from the endowment amount so as to see the effect of the endowment in action during their lifetime.

Policy #10. Personal Property. Gifts of art, furniture, books, stamps, coins, libraries and other collections must have their value assessed by properly accredited appraisers retained by potential donors for appropriate gift tax credit according to 1984 IRS regulations. The organization shall acknowledge receipt of such properties but does not have to verify values.

Such gifts must be acompanied by an endowment fund equal to half of the assessed valuation to cover insurance, maintenance, handling, storage, and other costs. Also, such gifts must be accompanied by a statement permitting the governing board to dispose of the gifts when they have served both the intent of the donor and the organization for a period of at least 10 years.

Policy #11. Real Property. Gifts of real estate — residences, farms, ranches, resorts, undeveloped, commercial — and oil, mineral, gas patent and other rights; and life insurance in existence or new life insurance shall be encouraged but costs of transfer, maintenance, etc., must be born by the donor. The governing board finance committee must be prepared to receive, hold, manage, and resolve such gifts to the maximum advantage of the organization including the retention of external managers.

Policy #12. Annual/Current Fund. The annual fund shall seek recurring, unrestricted/undesignated funds for current budget requirements. Funds given but designated for current budget features shall be considered as applicable to the annual fund but not supplementary budget allocations. These are funds primarily from donor income to organization income.

Policy #13. Capital/Asset-Building Fund. Popular usage of the term "capital fund" refers primarily to asset-building uses such as endowment, personnel positions, programs or projects, physical plant additions and/or physical plant modernization or alterations. Such fund programs request a portion of current assets, and/or a commitment of total assets in addition to donor continuity of annual fund support.

Policy #14. Planned Giving. Planned gifts are those philanthropic commitments arranged now but which will be fulfilled by one or more deferred gift instruments. Here, when a gift objective is requested for a named benefit to the donor, the donor may be requested to provide income annually from the eventual endowment amount so that the donor can see the purpose of the endowment functioning through life.

Planned gift devices are subject to severe IRS rules, regulations, and guidelines of the Conference on Gift Annuities. Therefore, there must be separate guidelines for each deferred gift instrument, including the consideration of declining to promote and/or accept those instruments which have high administrative costs and therefore low philanthropic productivity.

The institution must tell, sell, explain, and repeat information about the use of codicil amendments to existing wills and estate plans as a low-cost addition to existing wills and to reduce federal estate taxes.

Summary of Guidelines. The absence of such policies and guidelines for establishing gift and grant policies conveys an "anything goes" attitude. The very integrity of the organization is enhanced by the statement ". . . our governing board policies do not permit us to accept this particular gift offer." No organization can afford even the probability of being used or misused for philanthropic purposes any more than their accepting mediocrity or mere adequacy in its service programs.

All philanthropic gift and grant policies are subject to changing laws, rules, and regulations. Therefore, they must be reviewed periodically to protect present and future donors and investors and the recipient organization.

Code of Ethics for Endowed Investment Policies

Under the incorporating state not-for-profit statutory provisions, the organization's board of trustees is personally and jointly responsible for the legal management of a public trust on behalf of the citizens of the state.

Those individuals, families, and organizations who provide voluntary philanthropic gifts and grants in fulfillment of the mission, goals, and future plans of the organization must be assured of the confidence in the management productivity of their expected commitments. To these ends, the following statements constitute the endowment investment -policies to ensure donors/investors of the highest productivity of their interest in and concern for the organization.

Article 1. To inform all donors of the vision and mission of the organization since its founding, and of the way in which the governing board of trustees intends to use philanthropic resources effectively for its intended purposes.

Article 2. To provide the names of those individuals serving on the governing board with a brief description of who they are, thereby to expect the exercise of prudent judgment in their stewardship responsibilities and obligations in the management of all fiscal resources.

Article 3. To insure that such donor investments are being vested in the most respected and experienced investment counsellors for the highest possible, creditable income productivity.

Article 4. To provide statements of board-approved investment policies and procedures, studies, analyses, and requests to ensure the highest personal and professional integrity in the conduct of the counsellor relationship.

Article 5. To provide all requested audited statements of the financial conditions of the organization in all of its programs and services as well as administrative functions.

Article 6. To maintain absolute confidences and anonymity when requested.

Article 7. To provide name recognition as requested.

_____   _____ Chairman
Chief Executive Officer   Board of Trustees

                        Date

Board of Trustees
Investment Policy Statement

Section #1 — Endowment Fund Investment Goals.
The purpose of this investment policy statement includes, but is not limited to, the following:

1. to provide assurance to contributors to and investors in this organization's endowment fund that their gifted resources shall be invested and managed prudently;
2. to earn income for the programs and services of the organization serving the humanitarian needs and services of their community and society;
3. to the highest extent possible, generate long-term growth to offset any loss of purchasing power caused by economic insecurity; and
4. to use no more than half of earned income in any fiscal year for current operations, reinvesting the other half in the endowment corpus.

Section #2 — Investment Committee.
The board of trustees may appoint an endowment fund investment committee upon recommendation of and to serve under the board standing committee on financial affairs. Such investment committee shall consist of no more than three (3) persons experienced as business and civic leaders. The Chair shall be an active member of the board of trutsees and member of the committee on financial affairs. Members may be members of the board of trustees or ex officio members of the board without vote. The role of the endowment fund investment committee includes, but shall not be limited to, the following:

1. to select one or more custodians for the funds, resources, and securities provided and accepted by the board of trustees;

2. to monitor the organization's portfolio and resources on a regular basis;
3. to report to the board of trustees through the
committee on financial affairs;
4. to retain professional money-management counsellors experienced in not-for-profit organization
matters and to review on a regular basis their
compliance with stated goals and guidelines;
5. to recommend to the board of trustees through
the committee on financial affairs changes in the
investment policy statement.

Section #3 — Investment Guidelines.
1. The portfolio shall be diversified but should limit
its investments to common stocks; U.S. Treasury bonds
and notes; certificates of deposit in insured bonds; conservative mutual funds, money funds, etc. This is not
intended to mean that the portfolio must own all of these
forms of investment at all times. It is suggested that not
more than five percent (5%) of the portfolio (at cost) shall
be invested in the stock of any one company although
fifteen percent (15%) can be invested in a diversified
mutual fund. Excess investment in any one industry or
geographical region should be avoided. The portfolio
should also be diversified as to time of purchase of stocks
or bonds and as to maturity dates of bonds. The investment committee is admonished that the market and event
risks of investing in long-term bonds usually will outweigh
the higher yield normally available on these bonds.
2. Equity securities shall be preferred in seasoned
companies whose shares are regularly traded on the
New York, American or NASDAQ stock exchanges or
publicly available mutual funds. At the time of purchase
such securities shall be rated "B plus" or better by either
Standard and Poors, Value Line or the equivalent rating
for securities of financial or insurance companies.
Other investment opportunities shall be thoroughly
researched as to their realistic viability for potential

growth and stability in our ever-growing, diverse, entre-preneurial society.

3. No part of the endowment fund shall be invested in foreign securities contrary to United States government foreign policy.

4. Any recommendation for investments in acceptable foreign securities, private placements, short sales or margins, purchase or sale of options, purchases of commodities, real estate or financial futures must be approved by the committee on financial affairs and their recommendation for action by the board of trustees.

Conclusion.

This investment policy statement is offered as an intital guide, not a mandate, for sequential implementation. It shall be subject to constant review, revision, and updating as necessary due to both internal and external circumstances.

The board of trustees, as manager of a public trust, is encouraged to update guidelines and policies reflecting current economic and financial conditions plus changing and challenging investment opportunities to wisely accelerate the impact of endowment resources for this organization.

Stop Gift Club Abuses!

Who would believe that, in their pursuit of the vital budgeted gift dollar, some gift-dependent organizations adhere to such practices as:

1. **Discount philanthropy.** "Please become members of our gift-level clubs, but you need only give half of our minimum amount."

2. **Donor discrimination.** "Because your business does not have a matching gift program, you must

pay full price to become a member of our gift-level club."

3. **Two-for-one sale.** "When your business gives, we don't need your personal gift for you to become a member of our gift club."

4. **Buy one, get many free.** "Become a member of our gift club and we'll list all the names you want listed."

5. **Give once . . . forever.** "As soon as you reach a magic number of dollars by gift or bequest certification, we don't need any more philanthropic gifts from you."

6. **Substitutes are welcome.** "You don't have to make a gift of cash to become a member of our gift club. We can use hub caps or volunteer time equivalency credit for paying our salaries and energy costs."

7. **Where there's a will.** "We don't need cash for our annual giving and special project programs; just write us a letter stating that we're in your will and we'll make you a member."

8. **It's a pay-off.** "If you'll just join our gift club, we won't ask you for any other gifts."

9. **Insurance cop-out.** "Just take out a life insurance policy at any level with us as beneficiary and you will not have to give anything else ever. You'll be able to come to all athletic events, use our library, gym, golf course, parking areas, etc."

10. **Life clubs.** Recognition of donors by a life membership, which means give once and never again, defies urgent needs for regular gifts. Life clubs should mean giving for life and life hereafter.

Exaggerated? Not at all! An extremely large number of persons responsible for the implementation of philanthropic gift programs make such ridiculous offers — even though the purpose of a gift club is to attract dollars for urgent, continuous budgetary needs. And, in self-defense, these same so-called development "professionals" cite the names of prestigious institutions that follow such ill-conceived practices — as if to say that anything a prestigious institution does is sacrosanct.

Before discussing each of the above gift-club abuses, let's go back to basics. Annual fund solicitation exists to produce immediate dollars, not to produce numbers or lists of names! This productivity of dollars — gifts from donor income to operational income — relates to the budgetary support that is essential to provide for an organization's personnel, programmatic, and service needs. To insure the maximum cash flow into this system, each and every constituent must be inspired to provide the maximum number of dollars possible to insure fulfillment of the organization's mission, goals, and objectives.

Here are five basic requisites to the operation of a successful annual giving program:

1. Plan for and request philanthropic gifts from each and every constituent without providing any escapes whatsoever.
2. Create and sustain a quality program that reflects the highest integrity — highest ethics — on the part of the organization.
3. Treat each prospect equally, fairly, honestly, openly — without exception for any reason.
4. Increase donor gifts beyond membership club minimum gift levels.
5. Beware of plastic card membership payments, which block attempts to get donors to graduate to higher and higher membership levels.

To convince the donor prospect of your personal and organizational integrity, it is essential to eliminate any aspects that may make your program look as though it is an all-out attempt to get a "fast buck" by whatever means are available.

To ensure reasonable, honest, fair, open practices and procedures in promoting, accouting for, and crediting gifts, the governing board should adopt specific policy guidelines. Such guidelines should be the product of a special study of fair practices to all constituents. The use of truly experienced, objective, philanthropic management counsel can insure that dollar productivity is maximized, abuses of programs minimized, and both personal and financial integrity of the organization sustained.

Now, what's wrong with the nine abuses cited above?

1. **Discount philanthropy.** For example, a donor might give $500, have it matched through a business firm matching gift program, and the donor is then credited with a $1,000 gift and honored by membership in a prestige giving club. There are several unfortunate consequences of this method:

   a. Those donors who do not qualify for a matching gift are blatantly discriminated against, because they must give the entire $1,000 to be honored in the prestige name listing.
   b. In the minds of $500 donors, the credibility of the prestige club is tainted, the integrity of the program and of the organization is jeopardized, and an atmosphere of cheating is created. To the $500 donor, anyone whose name is listed in the $1,000 club is suspected of being a fellow cheater.
   c. The original intention of the business firm matching gift program was to increase individual giving by complementary generosity — not substituting for an employee's personal giving. Therefore, when an organization "discounts" the individual's gift, that organization undermines and violates the whole matching gift concept.
   d. The matched gift is a business firm gift that results from a company policy to assist organizations in budgetary needs. The company employee has no part in this policy per se. Therefore, the employee cannot honestly be credited for the matched gift; it was intended as a business gift and is a business gift, plain and simple.

2. **Donor discrimination.** There is no doubt that the donor who must pay full price for gift club membership is being discriminated against if one or more

other members pay less. The full-price member — as soon as he/she discovers this procedure — has an immediate and severe negative reaction, not only to the program or procedure, but, more importantly, to the organization that permits such discrimination to exist. They then take the only action that personal integrity permits; drop the membership!

3. **Two-for-one sale.** For qualified philanthropic gifts, the IRS recognizes tax deductibility for business as well as for individual income. Even with closely held or family businesses, individual owners receive annual compensation from the business they own. Each — the business and the individual — is a potential gift prospect. Even in publicly held business firms, executives who are alumni of educational institutions, former patients of medical institutions or members of any nonprofit board or committee should not be allowed to "duck" their gift responsibility just because the business firm provides a gift to the organization. The two constituencies are totally separate, and our not-for-profit organizations cannot afford two-for-one sales while their own budgetary needs go unmet.

4. **Buy one, get many free.** There is something wrong with a gift recognition program that permits a donor to make a single gift and then to receive multiple credit in an honor roll of donors. This sometimes is done only to swell the honor roll list. It's the old numbers game that even fools governing boards — until they must face up to budget deficits. Accolades of success are due only in terms of dollar achievement. It is not illegal or immoral for an organization to have large gift income from a relatively small number of donors! Furthermore, donors who benefit from multiple listings for single gifts know that there is something wrong. However, listings of spouses ("Mr. and Mrs.") for single gifts should be standard operating procedure because of the long-range benefits to the organization. For instance, when a spouse survives a deceased donor and has not — over the years — been accorded gracious recognition along with the deceased spouse, the survivor has little

reason to continue annual giving or to make a planned gift from the estate.

5. **Give one . . . forever.** Some organizations make an offer such as, "As soon as your annual gift totals $10,000, you become a life member." When such an offer is made, it relieves the person from any further obligation to give to the organization as soon as the gift plateau is reached. Any knowledgeable donor knows that this is merely an empty ploy to get X dollars. The donor knows that organizational budgets will continue to rise and that the organization will continue to have needs long after this total amount has been reached. And, therefore, good reason exists to suspect the quality of management of the organization.

6. **Substitutes for immediate cash are welcomed.** Gifts-in-kind should not relieve any donor from making personal and business gifts of cash just so the contributions will place the donor in a larger gift category. The abuse of gift-in-kind credit is rampant. There must be very strict guidelines as to just what such gifts are acceptable in lieu of cash. They should consist only of such gifts as are immediately usable by the organization in carrying out its mission and/or directly related to the operating budget. Every donor has a responsibility to share cash resources as well as materials — even if the gifts-in-kind serve to relieve the budget. There really can be no special honor in substitute gifts, but there is special honor in such gifts if they are over and above cash gifts!

7. **Where there's a will. . . .** Knowledge of the existence of a future income by bequest is welcome information. But future income is not current income, and current income programs must reflect current income sources. Many, many professed bequest provisions never mature because the constituent can change bequest provisions frequently. There should be a dignified and continuous program for the recognition of future-interest donors such as The Legacy Club, initiated many years ago by the author.

8. **It's a pay-off.** Giving generously to a prestigious gift club should not "qualify" donors to be excluded from being approached for other resource development programs, and no such offer should ever be made. As a rule, such an offer is a sign of organizational desperation — and the donor knows it. In view of any organization's multiplicity of needs, such an offer is a gross disservice to the organization.

9. **Insurance cop-out.** This suggestion provides a major reason for lack of confidence in every level of administration and governance. The nature of the suggestion inspires a $1,000 policy to get off the mailing list forever. Never would any charity receive voluntarily a one-million-dollar or more policy even for not paying for events and services. Charities should seek endowments now of annual gifts to insure that, at least, that gift can be income forever.

10. **Life clubs.** Given the diversity of assets, the suggestion that any size one-time gift would eliminate any other gift, asset or not, tells donors that executives and volunteers are fiscally naive. Gifts for life should be unrestricted, undesignated endowment income to insure fulfillment of the charity's mission.

Unfortunately, this malpractice list is not all-inclusive. Many organizations — if they look deeply into their own practices — could add to this list. But it is never too late to "clean up the act" by total renewal, redesign, and upgrading of the existing gift-club programs. The sheer weight of our national economy alone can force a study and upgrading of existing gift club programs if the integrity of the organization does not motivate such introspection.

But there is more! Two crucial factors should be built into every gift-level club program:

1. **Few minimums.** Through prospect research and constituent study, every gift club level prospect should be invited into gift club membership at the highest

possible level of the prospect's gift potential. There is no satisfaction in having a large number of donors at $100, $500, $1,000, or $5,000 gift-level minimums when many of these persons can be and should be (for the asking) donors of amounts far above the requested minimums, thereby complementing their interest in and concern for the mission, accomplishments, and potential of the organization.

Too, suggest gift participation in monthly sums at $20, $25, $50, $75, $100, $150, $250, $500, $750, and $1,000 — and watch the results. You'll be amazed at how easily prospects will consider monthly increments of these amounts. Potential donors can multiply 12 times the monthly increment, but let them do the multiplication. After all, we live in a monthly payment plan society. Why not express your suggested gift in monthly terms — whether the donor wishes to pay monthly or annually?

2. **Members in perpetuity.** If gift-level clubs are an important marketing strategy for motivating ever-larger gifts . . . and if your organization plans to "be in business" in perpetuity . . . and if the organization will need philanthropic support in perpetuity . . . then why not encourage your donors to *insure* that their annual gift will support the organization forever?

To each donor, suggest a **codicil amendment** to his/her will that will provide an annual gift income forever. (They won't think of this themselves; you have to make the suggestion.) Promotion of this suggestion should be continual, but an endowed gift must not be a mandatory condition for membership. In your honor roll of donors, use an asterisk, or a technique of that kind, to recognize donors who have endowed their annual gifts — and that will serve as a reminder to those who have not yet done so. When donors do decide to take this step, it is likely that their arrangement will provide for a larger annual gift than their present participation would indicate. Promotion of this idea must be ongoing and dramatized in creative ways.

The potential annual income from gift club programs can be far, far greater than that now realized. In a large measure, organizations have pulled the rug out from under the very income they need by creating programs which contain abuses and which impinge upon the very integrity on which the organization counts for even greater philanthropy.

⊙⫯⊚

To End

Not on This Board You Don't

You don't accept trusteeship lightly. You don't do so as a civic duty, a way to pad your resume, a chance to network.

You don't contribute of your time or talents or treasure lightly. You don't give to your organization just at the participation level, you don't abuse the gift-club system or allow others to, you don't visit the organization or attend its events or participate in its activities just when you have nothing else to do. You don't give until it hurts; you give until it feels good.

You don't assume that the CEO is always right, you don't depend on the staff as the only source of information, you don't read reports and spread sheets and minutes casually.

You do not take for granted that the organization should keep on doing what it has always done in the way it has always done it.

You do not leave it to board leadership to worry about the effectiveness, the accountability, the vision of the board.

On the Other Hand

You consider carefully and prayerfully before accepting a trusteeship.

As a trustee, you embrace the organization and its board, you give freely of time, talent, and treasure, and you urge others to.

You find out all you need to know to manage the organization wisely; you hold the board leaderhip and the CEO and staff accountable; you support and defend them vigorously when appropriate; you tactfully help make changes when necessary.

You are a joyful and persistent advocate of the organization.

Your trusteeship is included with your family and your career and your place of worship as a top priority in your life.

You hold yourself, the board, and the organization to the highest standards of personal ethics and public service.

You enjoy this heady responsibility, you have fun, you spread a spirit of positive enthusiasm for the important work you are all about.

⚝ *Appendix A* ⚝
Memo from the Management Consultants of Galilee to Jesus of Nazareth

September 1, A.D. 30

FROM: Management Consultants of Galilee
TO: Jesus of Nazareth

Thank you for submitting the resumes of 12 men you have picked as the managers of your new organization. We have run their profiles through our usual battery of tests and are enclosing the results.

Permit us to make a few general observations about the type of person you have selected. Most of these candidates seem to be of a rather ordinary type, not of the distinguished caliber we prefer for top management positions. Their character types and background do not seem particularly suited for the kind of efficiency, loyalty, and bold vision that your organization might demand.

We are particularly concerned about Simon Peter, the man you are considering for the leader of your group. Our personality tests indicate an unstable disposition. He is highly emotional, likely to be impulsive and overly enthusiastic when excited, but defensive or even given to ventilating feelings through cursing or weeping when under pressure. He has an exaggerated opinion of himself, the kind that thinks he can walk on water, but in reality is likely to sink like a rock. We tend to think that when his loyalty to you and your organization is tested, he will fail. A man like this is hardly the kind of foundation on which to build your church or someone you could count on in a storm.

However, we pleased to note great potential in one of the candidates you are considering. He is a man of talent, resourcefulness, and character. He meets people well, has many good contacts, in addition he has ambition and shows strong tendencies to fiscal responsibility. We highly endorse your choice of Judas Iscariot.

All best wishes to you and your new venture.

❦ *Appendix B* ❧
Governing Board
Resignation Form

Herewith I formally tender my resignation from the governing board of _____ , which is the result of considered contemplation and is an irreversible decision.

    The reasons I accepted nomination and appointment were:

☐ recognition designed to advance my professional, business, social position.

☐ no necessity to become an advocate for the organization.

☐ an expected honor for my other achievements.

☐ my ability to fend off requested obligations for access to my friends or funds or both.

☐ no cited obligation to attend meetings or otherwise support the organization.

☐ my ability to blame others for current problems not of my own making.

☐ I'm a great delegator.

☐ I can promise and not follow through.

or

The reasons I hereby resign are:

□ not enough ego satisfaction.

□ meetings grossly dull and boring.

□ no chance to know my peers.

□ no one asks me to do what I can do.

□ I never hear anything between stated meetings.

□ I was never told I would be expected to give money.

□ my business is dropping off.

□ I don't feel like I belong to a governing board; I don't govern anything.

□ I'll use any excuse to keep from giving money even though I approve budgets.

□ I don't know who the organization is or what it does.

□ my spouse is treated as a second-class citizen.

□ I was never given a letter or certificate of appointment.

□ I learn what's happening at the organization in the newspaper.

□ fear of being held legally responsible for problems not of my own making.

□ the board membership doesn't get advertised.

□ I've got other things to do.

I believe two-thirds of us should get out of the way of the other third.

Signed _____

Date _____

∞ *Appendix C* ∞
Some of the Who, Why, and How of Giving

Platforms for Giving	For These Reasons	These People Give	In This Manner	In Response To
Love of God. Love of fellow man. Sense of social responsibility. *Thoughtful, rationalized giving. In substantial proportion to ability to give.* The finer emotions. *Responsive giving — ordinarily modest, but wide-spread giving.*	To fulfill a spiritual conviction. To improve the quality of life. To meet a responsibility. To be fair. To set an example. To further an ideal. Pity — and sympathy. Generosity. Out of gratitude for good fortune. For a sense of spiritual elevation . . . satisfaction.	The deeply religious. Those who have a sense of social duty and have attained economic security. Those who are at "the edge of evening." The idealists and the visionary. *Who see the better tomorrow.* The creative givers. The outgiving. Extroverts.	After investigation and analysis of the need. Proportionate to the proper need. For demonstration and example. To provide "risk money" for new ventures. Impulsively — hopefully. *That an evil may be corrected.* Widely. *They have no pet causes.*	Careful and documented statement of the case. Personal appeal by a well-informed advocate of the cause seeking aid, or a social equal. Dramatized presentation. Continued information and cultivation. Identification — symbols.
Habitual or repeat giving.	Early training. *The family charity.* Habit. *Gave last year* Conformity. *Everybody's doing it.* Minor glorification. *Everyone enjoys esteem.*	Those who keep traditions alive. The responsive but conventional.	Regularly or intermittently. According to past patterns. Proportionate to the average giving.	Year-round reminders. Appeal made by same worker — year after year. Lists of other givers.
Response proportionate to the impact of the appeal on self-interest.	Fear. *Three out of four will die, etc.* Self-protection. *Don't let this happen to your child.* Self-aggrandizement. *Contributors' lists.* Submission to pressure. *Fear of social and business criticism.* Tax advantage. *Likely to increase size of gift.*	The fearful. *"Protect your home from . . . . . ."* The superstitious. *It's bad luck to refuse.* The socially ambitious. *Keeping up with the Joneses.* The noveau riche. *The best table at a benefit ball.* The go-getter in business. *Customer relations.*	Fearfully yielding to influence or pressure. After evaluating the quid pro quo.	Emphasis on dire results of NOT giving. Appeal by a social superior. Promise of publicity. *Memorials, honor rolls, and acknowledgment.* Statement of tax advantages.

© 1962 AAFRC

ᴈ Appendix D ᴄ
The Biblical Widow's
Mite Capitalized

For many years, I have been referring to the biblical widow as the greatest unrecognized philanthropist in history. She gave all the living she had, both current resources and estate resources. Who has given such total resources to a charity since? Further, the widow was a *woman*. Even today, women are characterized as minimal philanthropists in spite of their spiritual, verbal, and visual commitment to diverse charities. And, in the hands and hearts of women lie incredible philanthropic gift and estate potential.

A few years ago, as a faculty member at the Harvard Graduate School of Education Institute of Education Management, I referred to the widow as a total investor in the mission of her temple. A participant showed me one mite which he received during a recent visit to Israel. It looked like a piece of asphalt about two-thirds the size of a dime.

Southern Columns, the official magazine of Southern College of Seventh-Day Adventists, Collegedale, Tennessee, in their fall 1992 issue cited:

> The widow's mite (presumably one mite) would be worth $4,800,000,000,000,000,000,000,000 today had it been invested in a Bank of Jerusalem savings account at 4% interest compounded semi-annually.

Their math department interpreted this figure as four sextillion, eight hundred quintillion dollars.

I wonder if the widow knows about this!

৵ *Appendix E* ৵৹
Epistle to Donations

In the beginning was the "special gift" and the "special gift" comes first. The donor gave because he/she wanted to give and saw that giving was good. Whereupon it came to pass that college presidents (chief executive officers), treasurers, and in the later years, development officers throughout the whole land, dreamed dreams and saw visions.

They began to ponder questions such as, "what manner of mankind is this who giveth of his/her bounty so abundantly? And why is this so? Where shall others of like kin be found? And how shall they be moved that the fruit of their labors may become a joy and blessing forever?

Whereupon the elders and the workers in the vineyard took counsel with themselves. And they commanded the chief scribe to put down those things of which they were of one mind. So it is here written:

1. Mark well the division between the sheep and goats that the names of the chosen might be inscribed in the golden book of expectation whereby the nature and earthly riches of each may later be revealed. (Prospect master list.)
2. Wait not upon those of small means for there is little worth in it. (Prospect screening.)
3. Seek not gold for gold's sake, but search out those of vision as well as substance for their works can be a joy to themselves and to all generations. (Prospect evaluation.)

4. Know thy prospect as thyself, for if thou knowest the yearning of heart thou shall find their treasure. (Prospect cultivation.)

5. Ponder well the great needs of man and woman, for herein lies a key to open the lock of giving. Thus, it is written that "they must be a part of the greater whole." (The case or prospectus — in general terms of humanitarian service.)

6. Plan well and with courage, for David Burnham hath said, "Make no little plans, they have no magic to stir man's blood." (Comprehensive philanthropic goals — budget, capital needs, endowment.)

7. Know well that for which thou ask, lest thy words fall upon deaf ears. (The case, the vision, the mission, and specific goals for achievement.)

8. Think not alone upon what the prospect can do for thee but what thou can do for the prospect as donor. (Recognition or anonymity.)

9. Forget not that mankind giveth first to that for which he/she is responsible. Therefore, I say unto you, they shall be placed in a seat of responsibility that their gift may be a delight unto their conscience. (Cultivation — involvement.)

10. Sow well the seeds of confidence and desire in fertile soil and cultivate with patience for hath not one of the chief elders, Chester Tucker, said, "It doesn't take much time to grow squash, but it takes a long time to grow an oak tree." (Cultivation — continuous.)

11. Let a donor be surrounded by peers that their knowledge of the cause may be his/her knowledge and their good deeds, his/her good deeds and they shall be known as one of them. (Cultivation for continual and greater generosity — personal.)

12. Open wide the gates of the organization that the donor/investor may see its good works and walk with its people. And the chief executive officer shall lead them into high places, and the future shall unfold before them. (Constant cultivation — growth as investors.)

13. Shrink not from asking, for verily I say unto you, to him who asks it shall be given. (Cultivation — ask and receive.)

14. Wait first upon the trustees that by their gifts and their work, they may reveal the substance of their trusteeship to others. (First solicitation — gifts of confidence.)

15. In due time, several shall wait upon the prospect for his/her gift and they shall be peers, in high esteem; for it is written that thou shall not send a youth after a man-sized gift. And, that is why oftimes the chief executive officer is enjoined to be present, as the authority of that office is of no little importance. (Solicitation for investment — technique.)

16. Many shall write letters, but few will get results. But he who looks into the face of another and asks shall not be turned away. For as Alexander White, a worker in the vineyard for Harvard College, hath said, "Raising money successfully is like getting milk from a cow. You can't write the cow a letter; you can't send her a telegram; you must sit down beside her and go to work." (The act of solicitation.)

17. Let no bushel be put over the light of the prospect, but let the light so shine that it may be relit again and again. The Lord loveth a cheerful giver but he also rewardeth a grateful receiver. (The art of solicitation.)

Author unknown

❧ *Appendix F* ❧
The Philosophy of the Four-Legged Stool

Here is a different perspective on gift support for the advancement of an institution.

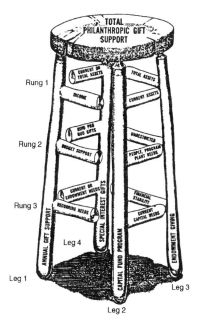

Leg 1 — Annual Gift Support: Recurring, basic, urgent, indispensable support from the donor's income to the annual income of the institution.

Leg 2 — Capital Fund Program: A supplementary gift provision from the donor's current assets to the current capital needs of the institution.

Leg 3 — Endowment Giving: A gift (through a planned gift device of some sort) from donor's total assets to the assets of the institution to provide long-term stability and security.

Leg 4 — Special Interest Gifts: Special, personal, business, social or economic gifts which do not fall in any of the above categories. *Quid pro quo* in essence, but more desirable.

* * *

Rung 1 (top rung): That portion of the donor's personal resources from which the gift is derived.

Rung 2 (middle rung): The use to which the institution puts the gift.

Rung 3 (bottom rung): The institutional need the gift fulfills.

❧ *Appendix G* ☙
For All Those Preparing for — or Recovering from — Meetings!

If God were process-oriented, the Book of Genesis would read something like this:

In the beginning, God created the heavens and the earth. The earth was without form and void; so God created a small committee. God carefully balanced the committee vis-a-vis race, sex, ethnic origin, and economic status in order to combine pluralism with the holistic concept of self-determination according to adjudicatory guidelines. Even God was impressed, and so ended the first day.

And God said, "Let the Committee draw up a mission statement." And behold the Committee decided to prioritize and strategize. And God called the process empowerment. And God thought it sounded pretty good. And evening and morning were the second day.

And God said, "Let the Committee determine goals and objectives, and engage in long-range planning." Unfortunately, a debate as to the semantic differences between goals and objectives pre-empted almost all of the third day. Although the question was never satisfactorily resolved, God thought the "process" was constructive. And evening and morning were the third day.

And God said, "Let there be a retreat in which the Committee can envision functional organization and engage in planning, be objective." The Committee considered adjustment of priorities and consequential alternatives to program directions and God saw that this was good. And God thought that it was even worth all the coffee and donuts he had to supply. And so ended the fourth day.

And God said, "Let the Committee be implemented consistent with long-range planning and strategy." The Committee considered guidelines and linkages and structural sensitivities, and alternative and implemental models. And God saw that this was very democratic. And so would have ended the fifth day, except for the unintentional renewal of the debate about the differences between goals and objectives.

On the sixth day, the Committee agreed on criteria for adjudicatory assessment and evaluation. This wasn't the agenda God had planned. He wasn't able to attend, however, because he had to take the afternoon off to create day and night; heaven, earth, and seas; plants and trees; seasons and years; sun and moon; birds and fish; and animals and human beings.

On the seventh day, God rested and the Committee submitted its recommendations. It turned out that the recommended forms for things were nearly identical to the way God had already created them; so the Committee passed a resolution commending God for his implementation according to the guidelines. There was, however, some opinion expressed quietly that man should have been created in the Committee's image.

And God caused a deep sleep to fall on the Committee.

— *Anonymous*

☞ *Appendix H* ☜
Nonprofit Organization Individual Governing Board Membership Audit

All not-for-profit organizations must be incorporated under pertinent corporate statutes of the state in which the organization is formed and or in which its headquarters are located. From the time its articles of incorporation are approved, the organization serves as a **public trust.** The organization itself, therefore, is a philanthropy. It exists for the love of humankind. Its destiny in serving its public and the public of the state lies in the hands and hearts of its governing board, commonly referred to as trustees — managers of a public trust.

Governing boards as a whole, and individual members, are seldom evaluated in terms of their commitment and function as a policy-making, not an administrative, board. The following questions are an attempt for individuals to assess themselves relative to their perceptions, experiences, and functions as trustees of a public trust.

Perceptions

	Yes	No
1. Before your acceptance to serve as a board member were you aware of, were you told of or were you shown a position description of personal and official obligations and responsibilities of board membership?	____	____

Yes   No

2. Were you given a trustee manual containing comprehensive biographies of fellow trustees and principal staff members; articles of incorporation, bylaws; mission and goals statements; last audit report; history and current facts of the organization?   ____   ____

3. Were you made aware of your up-front responsibility for continuing personal support of both budget and special fund programs as a governing member of a public trust?   ____   ____

4. Were you made aware that the governing board is a management not an administrative entity?   ____   ____

5. Were you invited or obligated to participate in a broad board and administrative orientation of all policies, personnel, programs, services, and state of the physical plant of the organization?   ____   ____

6. Does the organization have an up-to-date statement of its mission, goals, and objectives as a basis for a long-term plan for both services and fiscal security?   ____   ____

7. Is there a collation of previously approved policies available in a board operation manual or other ready reference device?   ____   ____

8. Do you really know and/or do you meet with each fellow board member outside of board and committee meetings?   ____   ____

9. Do you keep abreast of community, regional, and/or societal forces, issues, and trends affecting or likely to affect the organization?   ____   ____

Yes No

10. Considering your own personal talent and skills and your experience which you bring to this board, please indicate with an "X" your attributes and with a "0" mark your experience below:

___ ___ professional   ___ ___ real estate
         relationship   ___ ___ plant management
___ ___ management   ___ ___ public relations
___ ___ budget/finance   ___ ___ philanthropic
___ ___ planning   fund raising
___ ___ investments   ___ ___ government
___ ___ marketing   relations
___ ___ legal affairs   ___ ___ other: _____
___ ___ construction   _____

11. Do you sense or have you been made aware of personal conflict of interests in your role as a governing board member, between other board memberships, and/or other outside relationships?   _____ _____

12. Are the services of this organization consistent with:

    your own personal interest?   _____ _____
    the business thing to do?   _____ _____
    the social thing to do?   _____ _____
    a friend's interest?   _____ _____

13. Is the organization an indispensable asset in the community? Would it be missed if it didn't exist?   _____ _____

14. Do you have a letter or certificate of appointment as a board member?   _____ _____

Assessment of the Organization

	Yes	No
15. Can you describe at least three special strengths of the organization?		

_____

_____

_____

_____

16. Can you list the organization's three greatest needs?

_____

_____

_____

_____

17. Do you really know the qualities of the programs and services of the organization and the community's response to them? _____ _____

18. Are you pleased with the organization's:
    a. programs _____ _____
    b. services _____ _____
    c. facilities _____ _____
    d. communications _____ _____
    e. philanthropic support _____ _____
    f. investment return _____ _____
    g. other: _____ _____ _____

19. Are you pleased with the effective, efficient, and productive role of:
    investment counsel _____ _____
    banking firms _____ _____
    accounting counsel _____ _____
    legal counsel _____ _____
    other counsel _____ _____ _____

Board and Committee Meetings

	Yes	No
20. Are agenda and related materials sent in advance of meetings?	___	___
21. Do you read them right away?	___	___
22. Do they discourage your attendance?	___	___
23. Do you suggest agenda items?	___	___
24. Are board and committee meetings stimulating?	___	___
25. Should board meetings be held at places in the organization other than board rooms?	___	___
26. Do committee chairs report at board meetings?	___	___
27. Do committee chairs rely on staff members only for committee reports?	___	___
28. Would you prefer that staff members sit on the sidelines rather than with the board members?	___	___
29. Is attendance at these meetings a personal priority?	___	___
30. Are you satisfied with your attendance responsibility?	___	___
31. Do the same few members dominate all discussions?	___	___
32. Do chairs request participation of all members at all meetings?	___	___
33. Is time given to discuss societal forces, issues, and trends affecting or likely to affect the organization?	___	___
34. Do meetings emphasize policy matters for discussion rather than tolerate administrative matters?	___	___

	Yes	No
35. Is there an executive session for all meetings when board members can meet as board members including the chief executive officer without staff present?	___	___
36. Are there periodic retreats of board members facilitated by specialists?	___	___
37. Do chairs really preside or just open and close meetings?	___	___
38. Is the CEO and/or are staff officers too dominant at meetings?	___	___

Advocacy, Community Relations, Philanthropy

	Yes	No
39. Do your friends and associates know that you are a governing board member?	___	___
40. Have you hosted meetings of friends and associates on behalf of your organization? Have you been asked to do so?	___	___
41. Have you sought speaking engagements or other appearances on behalf of your organization? Have you been asked to do so?	___	___
42. To show trustee interest, do you feel obligated to attend the organization's special events?	___	___
43. Do you provide a generous unrestricted gift to the budget you approve as a board member?	___	___
44. Have you ever volunteered a truly generous philanthropic gift for your organization?	___	___
45. Would you be willing to solicit your friends and family members for gifts to the organization?	___	___

	Yes	No
46. Do you financially support programs in addition to budget support?	___	___
47. Have you volunteered to provide a bequest or other deferred gift device for the organization's fiscal stability and security? Have you been asked?	___ ___	___ ___
48. Have you volunteered to seek an investment gift or grant commitment for the organization? Have you been asked?	___ ___	___ ___

49. Have you contacted public officials on behalf of your organization's
- a. programs
- b. financial support
- c. other: _____

Have you been asked to do so?

	Yes	No
a. programs	___	___
b. financial support	___	___
c. other:	___	___
Have you been asked to do so?	___	___

Personal

	Yes	No
50. Is your board membership a source of pride, and is it personally fulfilling?	___	___
51. Is the board nominating committee recommending persons for appointment who truly enhance the value perceptions of the organization to the community by virtue of their influence and/or affluence as well as other criteria?	___	___
52. Do you nominate such individuals? Have you been asked to do so?	___ ___	___ ___
53. Can you really do more to help than you have been asked?	___	___
54. Does your spouse/family share your interest in, and commitment to, the organization?	___	___

	Yes	No
55. Is the board:		
a. too large	___	___
b. too small	___	___
56. Should there be an annual review for board member performance?	___	___
57. Should there be term limits for board membership?	___	___
58. Should term limits be rigorously enforced?	___	___
59. Should there be an automatic removal policy for members who do not attend at least three stated board meetings in any term?	___	___
60. Should the trustee emeritus status be reserved only for those members who have served the organization with evidence of great distinction?	___	___
61. Do you view your board membership mainly as a social responsibility?	___	___
62. Have you thought about what you would do if you were chair of the board?	___	___
63. Are you looking forward to:		
a. continuing as a member	___	___
b. resigning	___	___
c. retiring	___	___

64. What are your greatest rewards in serving as a trustee?

_____

_____

_____

65. What are your biggest disappointments in serving as a trustee?

_____

_____

_____

Chief Executive Officer

                                        Yes   *No*

66. Does the CEO serve at the pleasure of the board? ____ ____

67. Is there an up-do-date description of the CEO position? ____ ____

68. Is the CEO evaluated periodically against his/her job description? ____ ____

69. How would you describe the management style of the CEO:
    ____ manager of the status quo?
    ____ designer of the future?
    ____ builder of confidence?
    ____ team member with the board?

70. Being retained by the board, should the CEO be a voting member acting on matters of policy implementation? ____ ____

Number of years on this governing board: _____
    Beginning in 19 _____

_____
               Name of Organization
Date _____

❧

Bibliography

1. Books

Houle, Cyril O. *Governing Boards: Their Nature and Nurture.* Washington, D.C.: National Center for Nonprofit Boards, 1989.
Lawson, Douglas M. *Give to Live.* La Jolla, CA: ALTI Publishing, 1991.
Panas, Jerold. *Mega Gifts: Who Gives Them, Who Gets Them.* Chicago: Bonus Books, Inc., 1984.
Rosenberg, Claude Jr. *Wealthy and Wise.* New York: Little, Brown, 1994.
Rosso, Henry, et al. *Achieving Excellence in Fund Raising.* San Francisco: Jossey-Bass, 1981.

2. Periodicals

Advancing Philanthropy. National Society of Fund Raising Executives, 1101 King Street, Suite 700, Alexandria, VA 23314; quarterly, one-year subscription: $50.
Board Member. National Center for Nonprofit Boards, 2000 "L" Street, N.W., Suite 411, Washington, DC 20036-4907; published six times annually, receive with one-year membership: $48.
The Chronicle of Philanthropy. P.O. Box 1989, Marion, OH 43306-2089; 24 issues per year, one-year subscription: $67.50.
Contributions. P.O. Box 336, Medfield, MA 02052-0336; bimonthly, one-year subscription: $28.
Fund Raising Management. Hoke Communications, Inc., 224 Seventh Street, Garden City, NY 11530; 12 issues per year, one-year subscription: $54.
The Nonprofit Board Report. Progressive Business Publications, 715 Lancaster Avenue, Bryn Mawr, PA 19010; monthly, one-year subscription: $250.
Successful Fund Raising. Stevenson Consultants, P.O. Box 4528, Sioux City, IA 51104; monthly, one-year subscription: $120.

245

Index

What the Pros

"While every member of a nonprofit board will benefit from the wisdom in this book, Art Frantzreb provides special lessons in leadership for the person who now holds or may someday hold the position of chair of the board. Very little has been written in the fund-raising and nonprofit management literature about the singularly important role of the chairperson of the board. *Not on This Board You Don't* corrects this omission clearly and assertively."
—*J. Scott Buchanan, CFRE*
J. Scott Buchanan and Associates

"Few people in this country understand the role of philanthropy as well as Art Frantzreb. His extensive experience as a counsellor, his superb planning skills, his effectiveness as a communicator, and, most of all, his passion for his subject have benefitted many an organization. I am grateful not only for his wise counsel, but also for his willingness to share his accumulated wisdom through the pages of this book."
—*Adele C. Hall, board member of the Care Foundation and the Library of Congress Trust Fund, among many others*

"Art Frantzreb is the pre-eminent consultant on all aspects of nonprofit boards. *Not on This Board You Don't* is the best guide yet to making board membership an exciting, challenging, and rewarding philanthropic experience."
— *Douglas M. Lawson*
Douglas M. Lawson Associates, Inc.